JN440478

Strategic Writing and Essay Clinic

-A Structural Supervision to Essay Writing-

Hubert H. Pak

도서출판 BOSEONG 보성

Preface

This book has been written for university and college students who wish to improve the quality of their expression in formal writing tasks. It encompasses the creative essay, the question-based essay, assignments requiring research, and report writing.

Writing for personal pleasure is markedly different from writing for specific purposes dictated by external evaluators. Writing an examination essay or assignment requires a mastery of the techniques of writing and literature. To be really successful, students should also understand thoroughly the criteria by which their writing will be judged. It is not simply enough to set ideas down on a page. The clarity, structure and development of those ideas must also answer the purpose of the particular writing task.

For many students the criteria by which their work is judged remain a mystery. If essays or assignments are returned with a grade only, or very little criticism, it is difficult to improve future attempts. This book provides simple descriptions of the techniques of writing and a detailed exposition of the criteria commonly applied by examiners during their evaluation. It will assist people to develop writing skills necessary for a wide range of subjects and purposes.

Contents

Chapter 1

Understanding about Essays

It's virtually impossible to writing a good essay without understanding some important things about writing, and about writing essays in particular.

Understand about Essays

The aim of this section is really to raise your awareness of some important points.

* What exactly is an essay?

* Why do we write essays?

* How is an essay different from speech and other writing?

* Are all essays the same?

* What is the basic essay structure?

All of these points come up again in the book where they are treated in more detail.

What exactly is an essay?

* Some very important points about essays

- they are longish pieces of writing
- they are on a set topic or question
- they are structured - an Introduction, Body and Conclusion
- they include facts and information
- they include your own opinions
- they are formal
- they are not personal
- they support one point all the way through
- they do not include information on anything besides the one point

A basic definition

If we pull together the ideas and important points together, we get something like this:

An essay is a formal, structured piece of writing which makes a statement on a topic or question, and which supports this statement throughout with information and ideas.

Now, it is important here to break up this definition and have a look at it.

An essay is a formal ... (1), structured piece of writing ... (2) which makes a statement on a topic or question ... (3), and which supports this statement throughout with information and ideas (4).

(1) ***An essay is a formal piece of writing ...***

Essays are formal. The best way to understand what 'formal' means is to think that it is the absolute and complete opposite of the way you might talk with your close friends. It is not personal, friendly and casual. It is reserved, distant and quite serious.

(2) ***An essay is a structured piece of writing ...***

Essays are structured. Essays are quite long pieces of writing. For this reason, It is important that you structure your writing in the way that will best help your reader to follow you and in a way that he or she expects you to. Put very simply, you tell your reader what you are going to write about (the Introduction), then you write about it (the Body) and then you tell your reader what you have written (the Conclusion).

(3) ***... which makes a statement on a topic or question ...***

This simply means that you say something directly about the essay question. What you say depends very much on the essay topic and the type of essay. In most cases it will be a statement of your point of view on the essay question, but this is not always true. In some types of essay, for example, it might be simply a restatement of the essay question. Whatever it is, it is exceptionally important.

It:

- is the short, direct response to the essay question
- states one clear idea
- is generally one sentence only
- ties your whole essay together
- comes in the first paragraph (the Introduction).

If there is no statement like this, there is no essay.

(4) ***and which supports this statement throughout with information and ideas ...***

It simply is not enough to have a statement on a topic or question. You have to expand on this statement. Once you have a statement, you have to prove it, or discuss it, or in some way you have to elaborate on it.
For example:

- ... *I believe this because X, Y and Z*

or

- ... *I can explain this in this way - X, Y and Z*

or

- ... *here are some of the important issues related to this - X, Y and Z*

This is what the main section of your essay does. It supports and develops the statement on the essay question at the beginning of your essay.

In summary, there are four important things to remember:

- You must have one idea which holds your whole essay together from start to finish.
- You must make a statement about this idea at the beginning of your essay.
- You should not just write everything you know on the topic. Instead, you should choose information and ideas which help you develop your statement.

You must organize or structure the whole essay so that the reader can make sense of it.

What exactly is the purpose of an essay?

* Purposes

(1) Overall Purpose

The overall purpose of an essay is to ***convince*** the readers. You are not trying to entertain or inform your reader, but your overall purpose or goal is to convince your reader that what you are saying is right or at least a reasonable point of view.

(2) Specific Purpose

As well as wanting to convince your reader, you will have a more specific purpose which will be determined by the essay question. In most cases your purpose will be to argue the case, to discuss an issue, or explain something.

(3) Teacher's/Evaluator's Purpose

Teachers or evaluators set essays to explore your ideas and knowledge on a topic:

- Your ideas and opinions -what you think about a topic
- Facts and other people's opinions - what you know about a topic
- Extent of your knowledge - that you can use what you know to support and develop your ideas and opinions

When you write essays, you don't use same words or organize your ideas in the way you would if you were talking to a friend. For example, you don't talk about personal feelings and experiences in an essay because your purpose is to convince the reader. You need to sound sensible and objective and unswayed by personal experience. Also, you don not use slang or everyday colloquial language because we only use such language when we are speaking or writing to people we are close to.

Writing an essay is different from everyday conversation. In an essay, you need to choose your words and organize your ideas to be suited to:

- your general purpose to convince the reader and your specific purpose to argue, explain, discuss and so on
- a distant unknown audience
- the particular subject matter (eg. historical event, social issue)
- a formal written text.

Chapter 2

The Basics of Writing

Language, no matter how simple, has form. This form or structure includes word function, word order, tenses and the various rules of expression we call grammar. This chapter does not deal in detail with English grammar, but rather explains some of the basic elements which go to make up a piece of written work.

Words

A word has been defined as a 'conventional or arbitrary segment of utterance' (Simeon Potter, *Language in the Modern World*) and is effectively the smallest significant or meaningful unit of language.

Word Order

1. The verb normally follows the subject in English and, when an object is involved, it precedes the object.

   Thus: *The Governor has opened parliament.*

2. This order is inverted in yes/no questions.

   Thus: *Has the Governor opened parliament?*

3. The adjective usually comes before the noun it qualifies.

   Thus: *The famous actor appeared in the key role.*

4. Adverbs are less fixed in their placement. However, adverbs of frequency usually precede the verb.

   Thus: *I often run before breakfast.*

The position of the adverb is often determined by what the adverb modifies, for adverbs may modify a word or phrase or a whole sentence, In the following example, the adverb *generally* modifies the adjective *useful* and therefore immediately precedes it.

Thus: *Our visitors made themselves generally useful.*

Alternatively, the adverb may modify the statement as a whole and when it does this it can immediately precede the verb, or begin or conclude the whole statement.

Thus: *Our visitors generally made themselves useful.*

Or: *Generally, our visitors made themselves useful.*

Or: *Our visitors made themselves useful generally.*

Word Choice

Have you ever thought seriously about the number of words in the English language? Some counts go as high as one million. It is, however, impossible to give a categorical answer to this since our language is constantly changing. Professor Potter sums up this state of flux in this way:

> The making of words proceeds intermittently and unpredictably at various levels, national and international, literary and scientific, dramatic and poetic, serious and comic, rhetorical and colloquial.
>
> Simeon Potter, *Language in the Modern World*

This suggests that you should plumb the depths of your vocabulary more often and enlarge it. Writing which raptures the subtleties of meaning, which conveys exact shades of color, which imparts precision in definition is potentially very good writing. On the other hand, writers who tolerate amorphous words such as 'nice', 'good', 'walk' and 'talk' instead of the more exact 'delicious' 'entrancing' 'shuffling' and 'whispering', run the risk of thoroughly boring their readers.

The Sentence

This - apart from the word itself - is the primary component of the essay. One might define a sentence as a group of words which make sense standing alone. Thus: *He sat quietly.* is a sentence because it makes sense.
Likewise: *He sat quietly because the injury which he sustained at tennis was extremely painful.* is a sentence.

A sentence does not have to be short, but if you look at both examples you will notice they have the same opening clause which states the essence of the sentence: *He sat quietly.* This is called main clause, because it expresses the principal and most important idea in the sentence, and because it requires no additional material for it to make complete sense. Thus, a main clause may, by itself, be a sentence; but a sentence –while it must have a main clause –is not restricted to one main clause; it may have qualifying words, phrases or clauses added to it.

The Paragraph

A paragraph is a number of sentences held together by a common idea. Normally, the common idea is expressed in general terms in what we call a topic sentence. There is no set rule for the length of a paragraph but, as a rough guide, an essay of 400 to 500 words would probably contain five or six paragraphs.

Examine the following paragraphs, looking particularly for the topic sentence and how the paragraph is developed from it.

> People moved slowly then. They ambled slowly across the square, shuffled in and out of the stores around it, took their time about everything. A day was twenty-four hours long but seemed longer. There was no hurry, for there was nowhere to go, nothing to buy and no money to buy it with, nothing to see outside the boundaries of Maycomb County.
>
> Harper Lee, *To Kill a Mockingbird*

> A man stood upon a railroad bridge in Northern Alabama, looking down into the swift waters twenty feet below. The man's hands were tied behind his back, the wrists bound with a cord. A rope loosely encircled his neck. It was attached to a stout cross-timber above his head, and the slack fell to the level of his knees. Some loose boards laid upon the sleepers supporting the metals of the railway supplied a footing for him and his executioners - two private soldiers of the federal army, directed by a sergeant who in civil life may have been a deputy sheriff. At a short remove upon the same temporary platform was an officer in the uniform of his rank, armed. He was a

captain. A sentinel at each end of the bridge stood with his rifle in the position known as 'support', that is to say, vertical in front of the left shoulder, the hammer resting on the forearm thrown straight across the chest - a formal and unnatural position, enforcing an erect carriage of the body. It did not appear to be the duty of these two men to know what was occurring at the centre of the bridge; they merely blockaded the two ends of the foot plank which traversed it.

Ambrose Bierce, *An Occurrence at Owl Creek Bridge*

Its most remarkable quality was its rate of acceleration. In its palmy days the Model T could take off faster than anything on the road. The reason was simple. To get under way, you simply hooked the third finger of the right hand around a lever on the steering column, pulled down hard, and shoved your left foot forcibly against the low-speed pedal. These were simple, positive motions, the car responded by lunging forward with a roar. After a few seconds of this turmoil, you took your toe off the pedal, eased up a mite on the throttle, and the car, possessed of only two forward speeds, catapulted directly into high with a series of ugly jerks and was off on its glorious errand. The abruptness of this departure was never equaled in other cars of the period.

E. B. White and Richard Lee Stout, *Farewell My Lovely*

The three preceding illustrations all demonstrate well the art of paragraph construction, In the first example, Harper Lee's opening sentence, *People moved slowly then.* constitutes the topic which is then developed in the remainder of the paragraph.

In the second example, Ambrose Bierce gives a generalized statement about the situation in his opening sentence. *A man stood upon a rail-road bridge in Northern Alabama, looking down into the swift waters twenty feet below.* The author then proceeds to answer the questions we might ask: what has occurred, why is he there, and what is going to happen?

In the final extract, the author's opening *Its most remarkable quality was its rate of acceleration.* is filled out by specific detail in the sentences which follow.

All the paragraphs comply with the requirement that a paragraph be a unified piece of writing in which a single main idea is developed, that main idea being held together by a topic sentence. Further discussion on paragraph writing is given in Chapter 3.

Chapter 3

The General Essay

There are those for whom writing seems easy, and while the standards of excellence they achieve - apparently effortlessly - may be beyond the struggling writer, all of us can improve our essay writing. The ability to construct an essay and structure paragraphs for maximum effect can be learned; and once it is, the way is open for successful writing.

An essay should contain an opening paragraph. This paragraph should inform the reader what the essay is about, or if it is a narrative or descriptive passage, it should set the scene. It should be a fairly general paragraph indicating the direction of the essay. The middle paragraphs should deal with items of specific detail; while the final paragraph should be the natural culmination of the essay - a conclusion, a summation, a restatement, even a tantalizing challenge.

The Introduction

> 'The truly extraordinary man', it has been written, 'is truly the ordinary man'. The first time I met John Kennedy I was immediately impressed by his 'ordinary' demeanor - a quality that in itself is extraordinary among politicians. He spoke easily but almost shyly, without the customary verbosity and pomposity. The tailor-made suit that clothed the tall, lean frame was quite stylish. A thatch of chestnut hair was not as bushy as office-holders had portrayed it. He did not try to impress me, as office-holders often do on first meetings, with the strength of his handshake, or with the importance of his office, or with the sound of his voice.

This was how Theodore Sorenson began his eight-hundred page book on President Kennedy.

In some ways the introduction is the most important part of the essay. If a good impression is not created in the opening paragraph, you, the writer, are off to a very bad start. Essay writing can be compared to a dinner party: if the oysters served as entree are bad, the guests are going to be wary of the main course no matter how good it is. Time spent in formulating and constructing this first paragraph is time well spent.

The introductory paragraph has a special purpose. In it you introduce the topic and you seek to engage the interest of the reader. You may explain ambiguities in the essay question itself, or establish some necessary or useful background information. A good introduction can contain brief previews of the main points of the essay, map out the verbal landscape. Finally, it should contain a sentence in which your point of view or attitude for the essay as a whole is crystallized. This we might call the thesis sentence.

Read the following opening paragraph. Can you pick the thesis sentence?

> Life, we discover sooner or later, is a partnership. No man lives to himself. None of us is completely self-sufficient. We depend upon each other.
>
> The *Age*, 'A Saturday Reflection', 28 February 2006

If you picked the last sentence, you are correct. The preceding points are illustrative of the final one, and in the essay which followed, various aspects of 'being dependent' were examined.

Sometimes, at the very outset of your discussion you may feel it necessary to explain a difficult, ambiguous or important word. While it is proper that you do this in the introduction, it is equally proper that you do it both precisely and attractively. Consider this opening sentence:

> Capital punishment, which can still be used in Victoria, is when the prison authorities execute a man found guilty of murder.

It is, more or less, accurate, but it is rough, it lacks precision and in a sense is misleading. Compare it to the following opening on the same topic:

> Eleven years ago the last man in Victoria lo be executed was hanged. The state had had its revenge, a life for a life, and the due process of law had taken its course.

In this opening, capital punishment is explained but there is a finesse that is lacking in the first. Furthermore, the latter example starts the process of engaging the reader's attention.

Introductory Techniques

While there are a number of techniques adopted by writers in beginning their essays, there are two models which can readily be adapted to a number of purposes. In the first one, the discussion opens with broad, fairly general statements; the ideas then become increasingly specific until the thesis sentence is reached. In these examples the paragraph's thesis sentence will be in italics.

This is the opening of an essay, 'The Fragmenting Family':

> The institution of the family is under constant pressure in today's society. Once, leisure hours were mainly spent in the family circle. Now, there is a vast array of alternative entertainments directed at different age levels and pulling members in different directions. The generally freer society of today has conceded greater status to the child's peer group, while in the home television has become the mentor of the child and the destroyer of personal interplay. *However, the primary cause of fractured family relationships is the failure of the senior members of the family to adjust to social change*….

The other method might be called the contrast introduction. It is particularly appropriate in an essay in which the intention is to express a personal view about something, especially if that point of view modifies or conflicts with the customary one, like this example, where the writer opens a discussion on the good old days:

> Whenever I flip through the pages of a paper or magazine, or sit before my nine-year-old, 21-inch less than sharp-imaged TV screen, the virtues of car ownership are thrust at me. Even Channel 2 with its 'Torque'series has fallen victim to this independent suspension, power assisted, fuel-injected plush cushion phenomenon. The comfort of the ride, the speed of the journey, the sense of power, the prestige - all are qualities which, it seems, carry alone the bulk of the population and seem to symbolize this modern age. *But I hanker for the good old days-* the days when I was a nipper in a one-teacher school miles from nowhere it seemed, somewhere in Gippsland; where each morning my Dad harnessed a horse and I rode (without independent suspension contentedly to school.

In this opening paragraph, the antithesis of the writer's point of view is detailed first (the comforts of today); then the opposite, contrasting attitude, which contains the thesis sentence. 'But I hanker for the good old days', is reached.

Both examples would constitute good introductions. It would be possible, however, to improve the first by the addition of one sentence, a sentence previewing the main points of the essay, thus sign-posting its direction. Again, a word of warning: this can be done brutally whereas it should be done neatly.

To illustrate this point, consider again the first example. In addition to assessing the primary pressure on the family institution as coming from the family head, the writer effectively previewed the rest of the essay in the last sentence.

> The institution of the family is under constant pressure in today's society. Once, leisure hours were mainly spent in the family circle. Now, there is a vast array of alternative entertainments directed at different age levels and pulling members in different directions. The generally freer society of today has conceded greater status to the child's peer group, while in the home television has become the mentor of the child and the destroyer of personal interplay. However, the primary cause of fractured family relationships is the failure of the senior members of the family to adjust to social change. *They can neither keep up with it, nor understand fully the technology resultant from it, nor appreciate that the youth of today is educated to those changes, is better able to cope, and often intolerant of the uncertainties of the older generation.*

The three explanations of why the older members ofthe family are primarily the problem - they cannot keep up, cannot fully understand today's technology, do not appreciate today's youth - will then be taken up and developed in detail in three middle paragraphs.

These introductory paragraphs have form. They invite, they woo the reader to read more, they capture his interest, dispose him to the writer's point of view, and may, in general terms, indicate what can be expected in the body of the essay.

The Middle Paragraph

The middle paragraphs constitute the main body of the essay. Each paragraph should deal with a specific issue expanding or extending the idea or point of view declared in the introduction. In the example that follows, author takes up the idea of fires, alluded to in the introduction:

> There are two ways in which fires can originate in a nuclear explosion. First by the ignition of trash, window curtains, rugs, bedspreads, leaves, dry grass, and similar combustible material, as a result of the heat radiated by the explosion. Second, by upset stoves, electrical short circuits, and broken gas lines caused by the blast. The heat from a twenty-megaton air burst would be intense enough to start many fires at eighteen miles from the point of detonation. In an explosion on Columbus Circle it is most likely that, except for the Southern half of Staten Island, which is more than eighteen miles away and is partially shielded by hilly terrain, at least ten fires per acre would occur in every part of the city. Since the total area of the city is approximately 200,000 acres, one would expect well over a million fires to break out within half hour.
>
> Tom Stonier, *Nuclear Disaster*

Construction of paragraphs is extremely important in the body of the essay too. There are steps that can be followed to improve this area of writing. Firstly, a good paragraph is unified by a single main idea; it is concerned with one specific subject. In the preceding example, the single main idea is fires resulting from a nuclear explosion. This, a middle paragraph, should contain a topic sentence which indicates in fairly general terms the matter of that paragraph. Consider the example:

> There are two ways in which fires can originate in a nuclear explosion.

If the remainder of that paragraph is closely examined, it will be seen that the author has done three things. Firstly, he has explained in greater detail the subject of his topic sentence:

> First by the ignition of trash, window curtains, rugs, bedspreads, leaves, dry grass, and similar combustible material, as a result of the heat radiated by the explosion. Second, by upset stoves, electrical short circuits, and broken gas lines caused by the blast.

Following this, he has expanded and developed his reference to radiated heat:

> The heat from a twenty-megaton air burst would be intense enough to start many fires at eighteen miles from the point of detonation.

Finally, he has offered a pertinent illustration of the matter being examined:

In an explosion on Columbus Circle it is most likely that, except for the Southern half of Staten Island, which is more than eighteen miles away and is partially shielded by hilly terrain, at least ten fires per acre would occur in every part of the city. Since the total area of the city is approximately 200,000 acres, one would expect well over a million fires to break out within half hour.

Ways of Developing the Paragraph's Main Idea

There are then at least three ways of developing the idea expressed in the topic sentence: by further explanation; by expansion; and by illustration. In a longer paragraph, or if it is important to emphasize the main point, it may even be appropriate to reaffirm the topic sentence in a final sentence. Such is the case in the next example. Note, too, the manner in which the idea is developed from the opening topic sentence.

> The east coast of Australia has been blessed with a fairly equable climate. (*Topic Sentence*) Unlike parts of interior of Canada, the eastern seaboard does not experience an excessive seasonal or diurnal range of temperature. (*Expansion*) Despite the sometimes cynical laughter from Sydney-siders, Melbourne's rainfall, on average, is fairly evenly spread throughout the year, and in no month is it excessive. Furthermore, her winter temperature averages out a cool 52 degrees F. (*Illustration*) Thus, excepting the odd excessively hot or wet day, people living in eastern Australia find the weather much to their likings. (*Reaffirmation*)

In both of the previous illustrations the topic sentence was located at the beginning of the paragraph and if it is important to inform the reader of the paragraph content from the beginning, it is right that it should be first. Sometimes, however, greater effect, maybe gained, more tension created if you start with the specifics - the illustrations and observations - and end the paragraph with the topic sentence. This is particularly appropriate in narrative and descriptive writing.

> Over 100,000 spectators were gathered in the stadium. Skywards a high pitched throb, faint at first, grew in volume as the crack RCAF aerial stunt wing in fly-past formation neared the stadium they said could never be built. A crackle sounded as the public address system was switched on. All was ready. The 22nd Olympiad of the Modern Era was about to commence.

The better essays are ones which move in sequence towards the end. This implies that the paragraphs are well arranged and that they are in some way linked as in a chain: that while they are separate in some respects, they are nevertheless part of a whole. This linking process can be achieved by the use of appropriate connective words such 'on the other hand', 'nevertheless', 'moreover' or by the development of an idea only alluded to in the previous paragraph. Thus, the first observation made about the Montreal Olympics - the spectators - might become, in the next paragraph, the central idea, the topic sentence of which might read:

> While most of the spectators naturally came from Canada, colorful groups from all over the world were interspersed throughout the crowd.

By contrast, the use of the connective-word technique might link paragraphs thus:

> Neanderthal man was, in many respects, nearer to the ape than modern man. He was extremely hairy, he often as not went all fours, the top of his head angled sharply through scarcely any forehead to a protruding ridge we would call a brow, his nose was broad, flat and full-nostrilled, and his wide, animal-like mouth slid to a scarcely recognizable chin.
>
> *On the other hand,* Cro-Magnon man was noticeably human. His carriage was erect, his features more refined, he was less hairy and by his actions he demonstrated a capacity for reason.

The Ending

Earlier in this chapter, essay writing was likened to preparing a dinner, and the analogy was applied to the opening paragraph. The analogy also serves to illustrate the importance of the ending, for it too can enhance or mar an essay just as the dessert or cheese board can enhance or mar a finely cooked main course. The last taste lingers, and this is as true of essays as it is of food.

The ending, like the introduction, should not be concerned with specific detail, but with the topic as a whole. It is not just a summary - that would be tediously repetitious - but may be a summation that is, a generalized overview of what has been discussed. Or perhaps the ending may refer to the beginning, viewing the matter alluded to then in a slightly new light. Occasionally, it may be appropriate to end with a quotation or an unanswered idea for the reader to ponder. Above all, the ending must be interesting.

Compare these two standard endings of essays. The question was, 'What would be your reasons for accepting or rejecting an invitation to live on a commune?'

Ending 1

A commune represents to me the ideal existence and despite some limitations it would be the best place for me to live.

Ending 2

> Perhaps I am biased, but when my active, outdoor, extroverted son settles for commune life, which he would if he had the choice or more to the point, could find one (where are they?), I will happily visit for a brief weekend but then hurry back to the delights of suburbia.

The first example is quite unexciting. The second one, however, does attract attention. It balances ideas, savors words, and is attractively decisive in its conclusion.

The next illustration demonstrates how a writer might generalize a whole range of impressions - in this case gained while on a visit to Russia:

> And that too, I thought, as I sat down in my seat in the British Comet, was Russia. I fastened my safety belt and looked up to see the English faces of the crew calmly doing their work about me. I thought I had poem formerly ordinary, they were now suddenly full of the mystery for me, the mystery of a freedom as yet unknown in Russia. Suddenly, too, I felt myself to be so much lighter that I was almost giddy as with lack of ballast. Until that moment I had not known what a weight on my spirit had been the Soviet system.
>
> Laurens van der Post, *Journey into Russia*

It is not easy to have an appropriate epigrammatic quota-at your finger tips, but notice the effect when it is used:

> In his ninetieth year, the warrior statesman died. The world, however, would be eternally grateful for his rousing oratory and our literature permanently enriched by the numerous books this incredible man wrote. He was a man of indomitable faith and courage, and those nearest him should take heart from St. Paul's confident affirmation: 'O death, where is thy sting? O grave, where is victory?

The final illustration demonstrates the point of view that the subject under discussion is not easily resolved. There may linger in the last lines a tantalizing, tempting innuendo; an implicit thought to ponder on; a doubt; even a mystery.

> Evidence, then, strongly supports the view that there are UFOs. On the question of extra-terrestrial beings we are on less sure ground, for non have been seen by reputable witnesses. However, until technology advanced sufficiently, man would have been laughed at if suggested there existed tiny microscopic creatures we sometimes call bacteria. It took the combined talents of many men years to develop the technology by which they could be viewed, thus enabling the mystery of contamination and disease to be understood and explained. So the mystery of the UFOs still exists: we don't doubt their reality; neither can we doubt that somewhere exists an intelligence which created them.

This chapter has divided the essay into various parts. What should always be kept in mind, however, is that while you are constructing separate paragraphs you are writing a single essay.

Summary of the Structure of the General Essay

The Opening Paragraph

1. Introduces topic.
2. Clarifies ambiguities
3. May preview essay
4. Expresses author's point of view in thesis sentence.
5. Engages reader's interest.

The Middle Paragraphs

1. Each paragraph deals with one specific issue expressed in the topic sentence.
2. Development of the paragraph may be through:
   (a) explanation of topic sentence, or
   (b) expansion of implications in topic sentence, or
   (c) illustration of matter under consideration.
3. The topic sentence may be reaffirmed in a concluding sentence
4. The topic sentence may be located at the end of the paragraph to create tension.
5. Care in ordering and linking paragraphs is important.

The Ending

1. It may present a generalized overview of the essay.
2. It may relate back to the opening, viewing the matter discussed in a slightly different light.
3. An epigrammatic quotation may constitute an appropriate ending.
4. It is sometimes effective to end with a thought the reader is left to ponder over.

* An Example: General Essay

Outline three ways in which sport brings us benefits. (300 words)

Not everybody likes sport but most people agree that participation in sporting activity benefits us in many ways. The most obvious advantages are physical, but there are also social and personal benefits.

In the first place, all sport involves regular physical activity and, because of this, it helps us become healthier and fitter. Regular activity, for example, develops muscle tone and therefore improves body strength. It also fosters good breathing techniques and so improves our lung capacity. Furthermore, it reduces the risk of heart disease and high blood pressure. Also, because exercise burns up fat, sport is an ideal way to maintain a good body weight. This, in turn, is important for the prevention of other health problems.

Secondly, sport brings us many social benefits. Many people, for example, form strong and lasting friendships through participation in sport. It also teaches important lessons for getting on with others. These include sportsmanship, leadership, and the importance of teamwork.

Thirdly, sport helps us develop personally-that is, mentally and emotionally. One of its most valuable aspects is that it teaches us to deal with both winning and losing. Some people believe competition is a bad thing, but if it teaches this important lesson it can be extremely useful. Another personal benefit is that it provides an opportunity to set and achieve goals. For some people this might mean winning medals and breaking records, but for most, it means striving for their 'personal best'.

These are just some of the advantages of participating in sport. Most sportsmen and sportswomen probably do not consciously think of these benefits when they play sport. Like me, they play sport for one simple reason-it is good fun.

The Opening Paragraph

- Introduction

Not everybody likes sport but most people agree that participation in sporting activity benefits us in many ways. The most obvious advantages are physical, but there are also social and personal benefits.

- which includes:

• a lead-in idea (not essential)

• a statement of essay question

• indication to the reader of what you are going to talk about
  - an 'essay-map'

The Middle Paragraphs

- Main Body

In the first place, all sport involves regular physical activity and, because of this, it helps us become healthier and fitter. Regular activity, for example, develops muscle tone and therefore improves body strength. It also fosters good breathing techniques and so improves our lung capacity. Furthermore, it reduces the risk of heart disease and high blood pressure. Also, because exercise burns up fat, sport is an ideal way to maintain a good body weight. This, in turn, is important for the prevention of other health problems.

Secondly, sport brings us many social benefits. Many people, for example, form strong and lasting friendships through participation in sport. It also teaches important lessons for getting on with others. These include sportsmanship, leadership, and the importance of teamwork.

Thirdly, sport helps us develop personally-that is, mentally and emotionally. One of its most valuable aspects is that it teaches us to deal with both winning and losing. Some people believe competition is a bad thing, but if it teaches this important lesson it can be extremely useful. Another personal benefit is that it provides an opportunity to set and achieve goals. For some people this might mean winning medals and breaking records, but for most, it means striving for their 'personal best'.

- which includes:

- one paragraph per main idea

- topic sentences which tell the reader what the paragraph is about

The Ending

- Conclusion

These are just some of the advantages of participating in sport. Most sportsmen and sportswomen probably do not consciously think of these benefits when they play sport. Like me, they play sport for one simple reason-it is good fun.

- which includes:

• sums up content

• gives no new information

• gives writer's view of the topic in some way

Chapter 4

Understanding the Question

Why Understanding is Important

Think of an essay question as a set of instructions for a journey. The first task for the writer, as for the traveler, is to be clear about the instructions given. What direction has been specified? What territory must be crossed? If the writer has a clear understanding of the territory or topic on the one hand, and of the direction specified on the other, then he or she has the necessary information for planning an essay that will be relevant to the question.

The steps you are about to follow in the next two chapters concern the preparations to be made before any writing is done.

Analyze the Question

You determine what is relevant when you analyze your question. This involves taking the question apart so that its components, and then the whole, can be understood. There are two essential parts to a question: one is the *direction* part and the other is the *topic* part.

Steps of analysis:

1. Read the question carefully, several times.
2. Circle the directional words.
3. Underline the main topic words.

Examples:

(a) From your reading of his cases, describe Sherlock Holmes.

(b) What happened to the Tasmanian Aborigines?

(c) Who is the most important character in 'Lord of the Flies' and how much has he changed by the end of the novel?

(d) Capital punishment should be re-introduced. Do you agree?

Common Directional Terms

Here are some common directional terms that you will need to know:

Outline	Give the main points, usually in a sensible order.
Account for	Offer an explanation of how/why something happened.
How	Offer an explanation of/for something.
Why	Give the reasons for something.
Explain	Give a clear account of what happened and offer reasons for it happening.
Discuss	Give points for and against, based on evidence, and draw a conclusion from points presented.
Compare	Point out similarities based on evidence. (Some contrast may also need to be made.)
Contrast	Stress differences based on evidence. (Some comparison may also need to be made.)
State	Present clearly and concisely.
Comment on	Express a personal opinion based on evidence.
To what extent/ How far do you agree	Quantify your agreement/disagreement with a given statement.

Exercise 4.1: Analyzing the question

Using the underline and circle system, analyze the following questions:

(1) Outline the main problems that face Korea's biggest cities.
(2) Korea should have a new flag. Comment on this suggestion.
(3) Describe the journey undertaken by Columbus.
(4) Discuss the claim that smoking presents our greatest drug problem.
(5) Compare television news services with those offered by newspapers. What are the advantages and disadvantages of each?

Now review your analysis of each question:

CHECKLIST

- Do I understand all terms used?
- Have I isolated all directional terms?
- Have main topic terms now been made clear?
- In questions with more than one part, have I noted the directions and topics relevant to each part?

Where a question has more than one part, try allocating marks to each part. This method will help you to avoid spending too much time on one part of a question at the expense of another part. Remember that the marker of the essay will be using a similar method of allocation. In the case of a 'how and why' question, for instance, you could expect to allocate half the possible marks and about half the time to each part.

Question analysis is a vital step in the preparation of an essay. Now you have a system which can be applied to all questions. Use the system and be confident that you have dome the ground work.

Chapter 5

Planning

Why Planning Works

A plan is a blueprint for the shape, order and direction of an essay.

The great advantage of a sound plan is that it enables you to see what your essay will look like before you start writing.
Planning will help you to use your time more efficiently. Once you are used to planning, you will find essay writing a smoother process because you will have 'ironed out' problems and set your course at the planning stage.

Planning

A plan should be prepared for every essay you write. This applies both to research essays written over a week and to those written in class.

Each plan should be in *point-form*. It should be a 'skeleton' of brief points, which allows you to see the shape the essay will take. With a point-form plan you will be able to:

* list points for possible inclusion
* decide the relevance of each point
* decide the *status* of each point (i.e. as a paragraph topic or as an example)
* match points with appropriate examples
* check the plan against the terms of the question
* make changes quickly and easily
* give each paragraph a job to do.

It is of paramount importance that you understand the link between points in a plan and paragraphs in an essay. Each main point in a plan is expanded into a paragraph dealing with that particular idea.

Example 5.1

Describe Count Dracula.

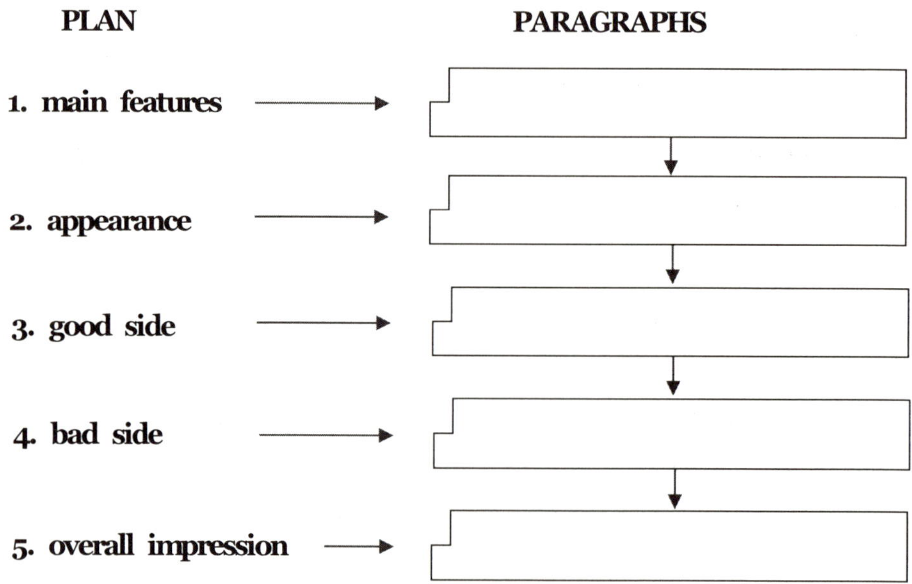

Note that the topic of each paragraph is never in doubt after the planning is completed. Much of the hard work has been done before the writing phase begins.

Planning Stages

The planning stages you use once you have analyzed the question are very important because they ensure the relevance of your essay and the order of its material. Each planning stage should be seen as a *careful-thinking operation*, and *the value of these operations should be reflected in the time that you allow for them*. Read each of the following operations as a thinking task rather than as a writing task.

- ANALYSE THE QUESTION

- SELECT RELEVANT POINTS
- DECIDE STATUS OF POINTS

Instead of waiting for the best or most relevant ideas to come floating into your head, try brainstorming. This first step involves turning over lots of ideas rather than only trying to come up with the best ones. It is important to start the selection process and to keep it going. Do not worry if a few ideas have to be discarded; it is better that the selection takes place now rather than later.

The second step involves deciding whether a point should become a paragraph topic or a supporting point within a paragraph. One method of isolating paragraph topics is to box them. When this has been done, arrows may be used to link the relevant supporting points to the appropriate paragraph topic.

Once the status of points has been decided, they can be ordered ad expanded upon.

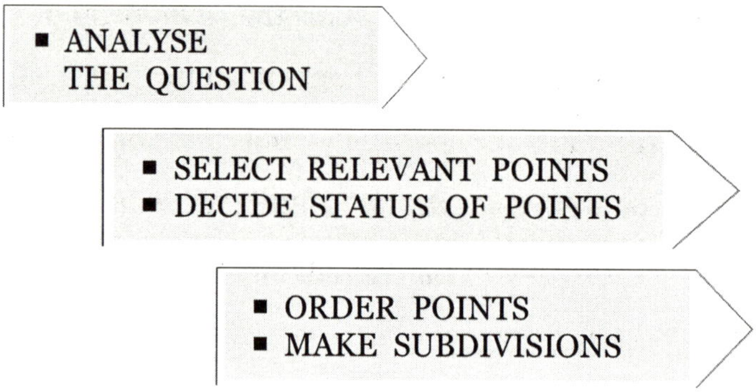

- ANALYSE THE QUESTION

- SELECT RELEVANT POINTS
- DECIDE STATUS OF POINTS

- ORDER POINTS
- MAKE SUBDIVISIONS

Planning a Descriptive Essay

A descriptive essay presents an organized word picture. It should make an impact on the reader's senses.

Descriptive essays may appear to rely on creativity rather than on planning for their impact, but the principle of careful planning is still needed if an essay is to be relevant and clear in its description.

Look at the following example of a descriptive essay plan. What particular organizational tasks are evident in this plan?

Example 5.2

Describe the scene from your window.

POINTS FOR SELECTION	ORDERED PARAGRAPH TOPICS	SUBDIVISIONS
~~grass~~		
sky		sky
sights	1 sights	gardens
gardens		moving things
buildings		buildings
moving things		
bird noises		bird noises
sounds	2 sounds	children's voices
children's voices		sheep bleating
sheep bleating		
~~fences~~		
flower scents		flower scents
smells	3 smells	cut grass
cut grass		cooking smells
cooking smells		

Exercise 5.1 : Planning

Prepare a plan for each of the following descriptive essay questions:

(1) Describe a beach scene.

(2) Describe Santa Claus.

In planning for each essay, use the method demonstrated to:

- ▪ ANALYSE THE QUESTION
- ▪ SELECT RELEVANT POINTS
- ▪ DECIDE STATUS OF POINTS
- ▪ ORDER POINTS
- ▪ MAKE SUBDIVISIONS

You may refer to precious examples and definitions as often as you wish. Be prepared to make changes. This is an important part of the planning process.

Use the headings 'points for selection', 'ordered paragraph topics' and 'subdivisions' as a reminder of the planning stages.

Now review each plan:

CHECKLIST

- Have I thoroughly analyzed the question?
- Are my subdivisions more specific than my paragraph topics?
- Are my paragraph topics in a logical order?
- Have I tested the plan against the terms of the question?
- Have I made changed to produce a better plan?

When you write your essay, you will be guided by the 'skeleton' that you make in your plan. Always plan before you write, even for the simplest of questions

****Keep each of your plans for use in the writing phase****

Chapter 6

Writing

Why Structure Is Vital

Before you begin writing your essay, you should be prepared to:

- **Write for a particular audience**
- **Write to plan**
- **Draft your written response**

Write for a particular audience

All writers have an obligation to see that what they write is appropriate for their intended audience. School essays are mostly written for an *informed* audience. An informed audience will know the material and will be more interested in your comments, observations and interpretation rather than in you ability to re-tell stories or summarize events.

Write to plan

Once you are satisfied that your plan provides a sound framework for your written response to a question, you must follow that plan. Although it may seem awkward at first, writing to a plan makes the writing task easier because there are clear steps to follow. It is also safer, because you can test the relevance of your answer before you begin to write the essay.

Draft your written response

During the writing phase of essay construction, your plan is translated into paragraphs. Read the following section on drafting and decide for yourself the importance of the drafting process.

Drafting

A draft is a particular version of a piece of writing. Drafting is the process of writing and then re-writing. This process of making changes ensures that the writer's intended meaning is conveyed more clearly and simply.

When you write an essay under test conditions, you are unlikely to have the time to do more than one draft. This makes the plan all the more critical. However, when you are allowed several days to write an essay, it will be expected that your finished product will have been carefully drafted.

The drafted paragraph below is an introduction to a descriptive essay answering the question 'Describe Count Dracula'. Look carefully at the changes that have been made to the original draft.

Example 6.1

FIRST DRAFT

Count Dracula ~~*was an expert at concealing the truth*~~.

(sophistication)

He impressed people with his ~~*manners*~~ and his apparent

(everyone)

good will towards ~~*his victims*~~. He fooled the victims

(of his nature)

with this good side^ ~~*and they realized this too late.*~~

(action)

He was driven to^ ~~*kill*~~ by the dark side of his character, which dominated him.

SECOND DRAFT

sophisticated appearance,

Count Dracula impressed people with his^ ~~*sophistication*~~

and ~~his apparent good will towards everyone. He fooled~~

the

~~*the victims*~~ with ~~*this*~~ good side of this nature, ~~*and*~~ he

won their trust. ~~*He was driven to action by*~~ ~~the~~ dark

drove him to action and

side of his character,^ ~~*which*~~ dominated him.

THIRD DRAFT

Count Dracula impressed people with his ~~*sophisticated*~~

however, it was the

appearance, and with the good side of his nature ~~he~~.^

that dominated and

[won their trust.] ~~*The*~~ bad side^ ~~*of*~~ his character^ drove

him to action ~~*and dominated him.*~~

FINAL DRAFT

Count Dracula impressed people with his appearance, and won their trust with the good side of his nature. However, it was the bad side that dominated his character and drove him to action.

Find examples of the following changes :

◆ to insert ◆ to re-order ◆ to delete (i.e: take out) ◆ to clarify

Paragraphs that will probably require the most drafting are the *introduction* and *conclusion*.

Translating Your Plan into Paragraphs

There are three types of paragraph that you must be able to use in formal essays. Each of these has a specific function in terms of the type of information that it presents to the reader.

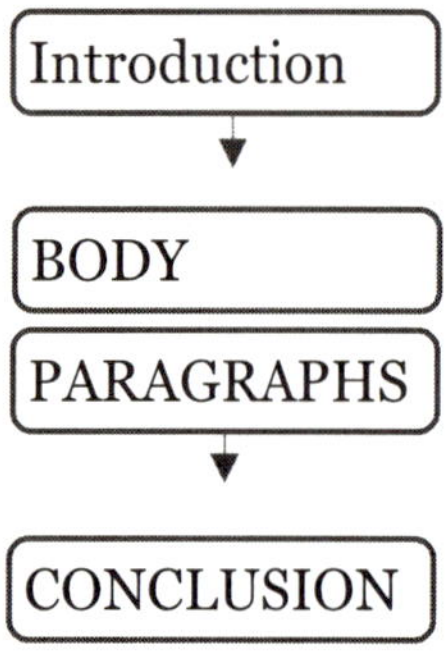

Introduction	This tells the reader the direction that the essay will take.
BODY PARAGRAPHS	Each body paragraph deals with a topic by expanding, supporting and commenting on it.
CONCLUSION	This paragraph sums up what has been said in response to the question.

Each type of paragraph will be examined in detail in the following pages. As you read each section, ask yourself how important the plan has become by this stage, and whether a well-prepared plan makes the writing task easier.

The plans that you prepared in exercise 5.1 will be required during this section, beginning with plan (1). This will be your chance to see how your careful thinking in the planning phase will pay off when it comes to constructing the paragraphs.

The Introduction

■ SET DIRECTIONS

An introduction is your first contact with the reader. It should tell the reader where you are about to take him or her, just as a signpost directs travelers.

An introduction should:

* capture the reader's attention
* warn the reader of the main points to be made in later paragraphs (i.e. paragraph topics)
* warn the reader of the particular approach adopted towards the subject of the essay
* set a clear direction in response to the terms of the question
* end when the job is done.

An introduction should not:

* ramble
* start a discussion (body paragraphs will do this where necessary)
* ignore the terms of the question
* mention specific examples or state facts
* confuse the reader.

Example 6.2

Describe Count Dracula.

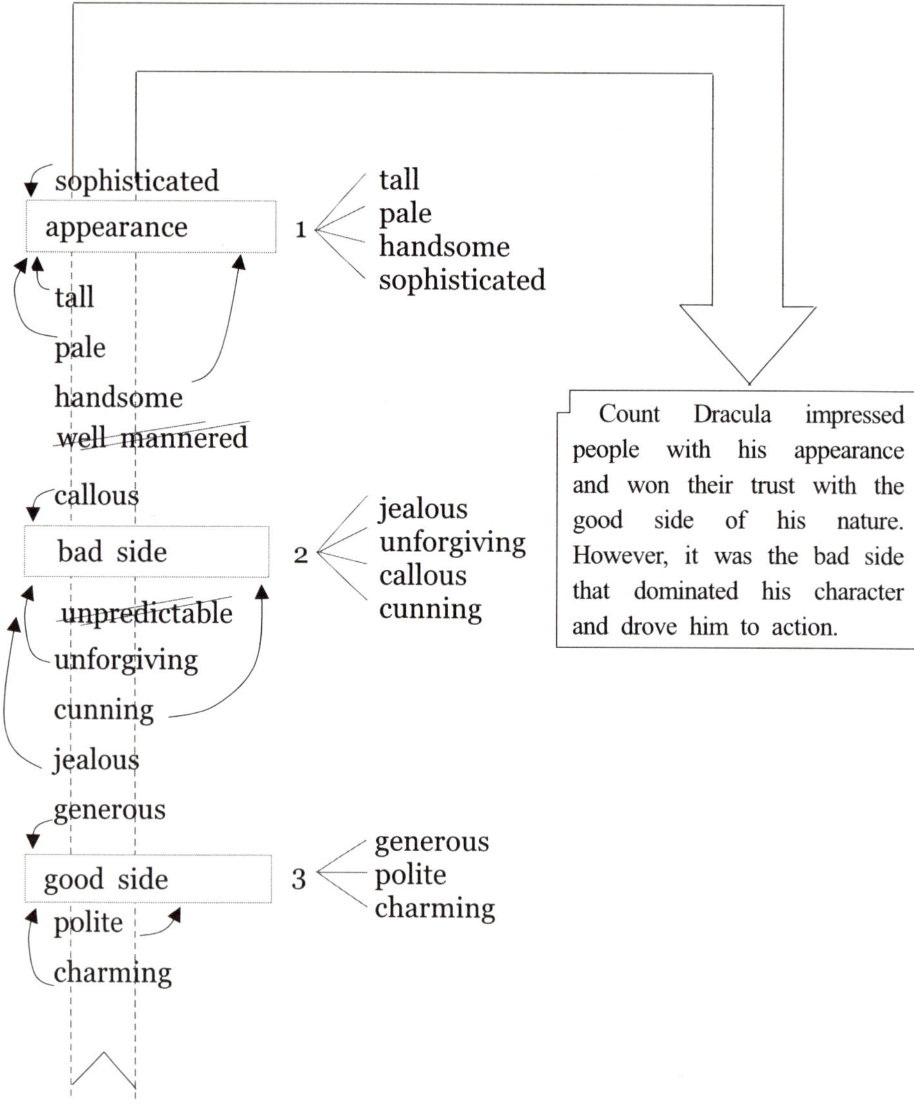

Has this introduction *set a clear direction* for the reader to follow? Have you been warned what to expect in the body paragraphs? Read the paragraph through carefully. Have specific details been included? Check the plan for differences between paragraph topics and subdivisions. Look, for instance, at the difference between 'appearance' and 'tall'. Only paragraph topics should have contributed to this introduction; the subdivisions or specific details, 'tall', 'jealous' and so on, must be left for the body paragraphs.

With so much important information to be transmitted through the introduction, you can understand why *clarity of expression* is essential. Never be afraid to use short sentences to ensure that your intention is clear. You want your reader to follow you into the body paragraphs.

The length of each introduction may vary according to the length of the essay, but as a general rule, four to six lines should be sufficient for most essays.

Exercise 6.1: Drafting an introduction

Examine the plans that you drafted in exercise 4.1. Take special note of the paragraph topics. Now draft an introduction from plan number (1). Take your time; this is a *method* exercise. You may do as many drafts as you wish.

Remember: Set Directions

Now review your introduction:

CHECKLIST

- Have I given the reader a clear direction to follow?
- Have I warned the reader of the main subdivisions within my essay?
- Has my expression been clear, concise and to the point?
- As a reader, do I feel ready to go on?

** **Keep your plan and introduction together for use in exercise 5.2.** **

The Body Paragraphs

- SET DIRECTIONS

  - EXPAND
  - SUPPORT
  - LINK

Each body paragraph is based on a topic prepared for in your plan. It must also fit into the essay's sequence of paragraphs by making links with the question and with other paragraphs.

A body paragraph should:

* expand on its topic using the minor subdivisions
* support its topic with specific details and/or examples
* make links with the question and with other paragraphs.

A body paragraph should not:

* ramble
* stray from its planned topic
* ignore the directional terms of the question
* deal with material outside the terms of the question, no matter how interesting it may be.

When beginning a paragraph, your first step is to write the *topic sentence.* The topic sentence tells the reader what the paragraph will be about. It is usually the first sentence in a paragraph. The topic sentence is underlined in example 5.3.

Example 6.3

Match this with example 6.2.

PLAN

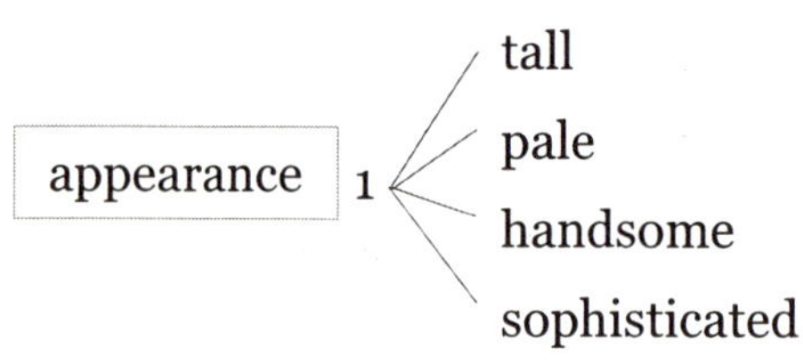

BODY PARAGRAPH

The Count's appearance always had a favorable impact on people. He was tall and carried himself well. His skin was quite pale but this helped to highlight his handsome profile. Perhaps the strongest feature of Dracula's appearance was his sophisticated bearing. It was this demonstration of good breeding that did most to set people at ease in his company.

The topic sentence in a body paragraph is simple to construct. All the writer has to do is to take the paragraph topic from the plan and convert this to a sentence. This topic sentence should be worded in fairly general terms because it serves as an introduction to the paragraph. Does the above example illustrate this? Look at the difference between 'favorable' and 'handsome', for instance.

Now study the remainder of the paragraph. Does it keep strong links with the plan? Are points in the plan treated in the same order in the paragraph? What sort of job does the final sentence do for this paragraph? Discuss our responses to these questions with other students.

Example 6.4

Match this with example 5.2.

PLAN

BODY PARAGRAPH

The topic sentence begins the paragraph.

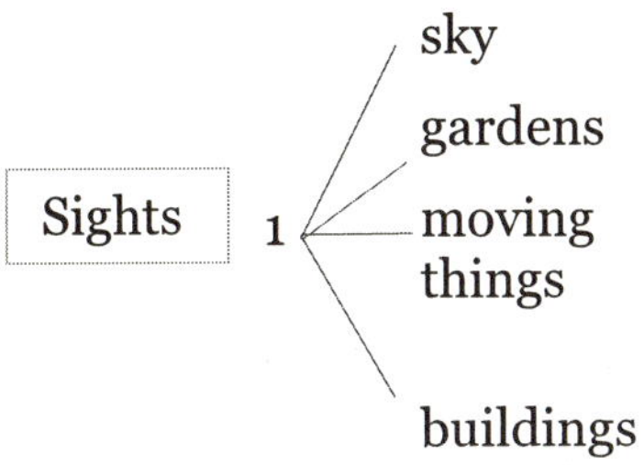

Sights 1

- sky
- gardens
- moving things
- buildings

Whatever the season, the sights to be seen from my window are always colourful. The sky dominates the picture with its baked-enamel blues and whites. Gardens paint bright islands of reds and yellows, and provide a border to the scene. The cows, sheep and people all seem to move by in a lazy, satisfied way. All buildings within sight are of shiny red corrugated iron which belies their age. The scene is always bright, but it is also ordered and peaceful.

This comment concludes the paragraph.

The points from the plan are used in the same order in the body paragraph. The topic sentence sets the direction for the paragraph using comparatively general terms. (Note that 'colorful' is more general than 'baked-enamel blues' and 'shiny red'.)

The bulk of a body paragraph should be spent dealing with the specific details set out in the plan, but the *intention* of the paragraph should never be forgotten. It is the topic sentence that reminds the writer of this intention.

The final sentence of the paragraph in example 5.4 is different from the preceding sentences. It sums up what the paragraph has said and *links* the paragraph with the question by way of a concluding comment. Each body paragraph's comment will be important when it is time to write the conclusion of the essay.

Now read both paragraphs again. Have the topics been *expanded*? Have they been *supported* with specific examples? Finally, have the paragraphs been *linked* to the question? Find evidence to support your response in each case.

Exercise 6.2: Drafting body paragraphs

For this exercise you will need your plan and introduction from exercise 5.1. Reread each of them before you begin.

Your task here is to expand your plan into body paragraphs. Most of the hard work has already been done in the plan. Feel free to go back to any definitions or examples that may be of use.

Remember: Expand; Support; Link.

Now review your body paragraphs:

CHECKLIST

- Is the topic of each paragraph made clear at the outset?
- Have all the subdivisions of the plan been translated into the text of the paragraphs?
- Has my final sentence in each paragraph rounded off the paragraph?

** **Keep your plan, introduction and body paragraphs together for use in exercise 6.3.** **

The Conclusion

■ SET DIRECTIONS

▪ EXPAND
▪ SUPPORT
▪ LINK

▪ TIE TOGETHER
▪ SUM UP
▪ MAKE JUDGEMENTS

The conclusion is even more important than the introduction as it draws together the threads of the essay to arrive at some useful outcome or judgment. This summing up must respond directly to the terms of the question. To do this, you, the writer, must weigh up and tie together the concluding comments of each paragraph. Remember, you concluding paragraph must satisfy the reader that you have understood, thought about, and fully answered the question.

A conclusion should:

* tie together comments made earlier in the text of the essay
* sum up what has been said in response to the terms of the question, particularly where more than one point of view is involved
* make judgments that carry some weight and that are within the terms of the question

* show some insights into the topic written about.

A conclusion should not:

* be a re-worded introduction
* continue a discussion
* bring in new material or supporting evidence. (This is not to say that we should rule out the suggestion of new alternatives or hint at new directions in a conclusion. Conclusions should allow such suggestions as long as these are consistent with the preceding text.)

You will find most of the material for the conclusion in the comments that you have made in the body of the essay. If you find conclusions difficult to write, it may be that you have not been commenting on points made in the body paragraphs.

Perhaps one of the most satisfying characteristics of a good conclusion is that it reflects an original way of looking at things. It is this original response to a question which shows the reader that the writer has been prepared to think things through.

Example 6.5

Match this with examples 6.2 and 6.3.

CONCLUSION

This statement briefly summarizes what the essay has shown.

This statement is a general observation that can now be made.

The final sentence gives the reader a verdict or decision that is consistence with the question.

Dracula was certainly a strange figure. He represented the best and worst in man, but these extremes were not in balance.
His goodness was only skin-deep, while his heart was black and cold. Dracula, the man, was only a shell covering the fiend within.

Look back at the introductory paragraph in example 5.2. How is the introduction different from the conclusion? Are the two paragraphs interchangeable? How important are the points made in the conclusion? Do these points leave the reader satisfied that the question has been answered? Think about these questions as you follow example 6.6.

Example 6.6

Match this with examples 5.2 and 6.4.

CONCLUSION

This statement sums up what has been said in the body paragraphs.

This final sentence rounds off the paragraph with two clear observations about the scene.

> This scene draws the observer into a slow, timeless world. All sensory information is natural and without discord.
> The scene is thus one of natural harmony, and its effect is to leave the beholder at peace.

What things are said here that would not be appropriate in the introduction? Does this conclusion *tie together* the main threads explored earlier in examples 5.2 and 6.4? (For instance, are sights, sounds and smells drawn together by one comment?) Does it *sum up* what has been shown? Finally, has the writer been able to answer the question? For instance, what sort of scene is it, and what has been the effect on the observer?

Exercise 6.3: Drafting the conclusion

For this exercise, you will need the plan, introduction and body paragraphs from exercise 6.2. Reread all of you paragraphs before you begin.

Your task is to draft the conclusion, the most important paragraph of the essay.

Remember: Tie together; Sum up; Make judgments

Now review your conclusion:

CHECKLIST

- Have I tied together comments made in the body paragraphs?
- Where necessary, have I weighed alternative views against each other?
- Have I summed up what has been said in the essay?
- Have I given the reader an interesting and useful answer to the question?

Putting It All Together

You should be able to read an essay as a united whole, rather than as a jumble of component pieces. Keeping this in mind, read the two completed essays that follow.

1. Describe Count Dracula

Count Dracula impressed people with his appearance and won their trust with the good side of his nature. However, it was the bad side that dominated his character and drove him to action.

The Count's appearance always had a favorable impact on people. He was tall and carried himself well. His skin was quite pale but this helped to highlight his handsome profile. Perhaps the strongest feature of Dracula's appearance was his sophisticated bearing. It was this air of good breeding that did most to set people at ease in his company.

Most observers saw Dracula as a good-natured man. He was unfailingly polite when introduced to people and he gave the impression that he was a socialite whose role in life was to give pleasure to others. Ladies always found him to be a charming host; men felt that their wives and daughters were safe in his hands. Dracula showed his support for charities, particularly for the Red Cross Blood Bank. Here, it seemed, was one of the true gentlemen of Europe.

Survivors told of the darker side of the man's nature. While he charmed the women, he was insanely jealous of competition and frequently murdered young men who posed a threat to his influence. Those who were critical or disloyal were eventually lured to ghastly fates. This cruel and cunning mind was the last thing people expected of Dracula, but his victims soon discovered that it was only a veneer of civilization which covered Europe's greatest monster.

Dracula was certainly a strange figure; he represented the best and the worst in man, but these extremes were not in balance. His goodness was only skin-deep, while his heart was black and cold. Count Dracula, the man, was but a shell covering the fiend within.

2. Describe the scene from your window.

There is much to sense from my window. The sights are colorful, the sounds are soothing and the smells are intoxicating. Throughout the year, the scene is pleasantly peaceful for all who are fortunate enough to be part of it.

Whatever the season, the sights to be seen from my window are always colorful. The sky dominates the picture with its baked-enamel blues and whites. Gardens paint bright islands of reds and yellows, and provide a border to the scene. The cows, sheep and people all seem to move by in a lazy, satisfied way. All buildings within sight are of shiny red corrugated iron which belies their age. The scene is always bright, ordered and peaceful.

All sounds reaching my room have a soothing effect on the listener. The finches, wrens and magpies are there to wake the household with their exuberant morning calls. Children's voices come floating across from the swings in the pine trees, their giggles ripping out over the paddocks. Sheep bleat contentedly in the background or call lazily to their lambs. These sounds reflect a slow pace of life in a natural environment.

A subtle but intoxicating range of scents is the most powerful aspect of the scene. Rose perfumes drift through the house and cure any staleness lingering there. Outside, the scent of cut grass sweetly recommends itself to all. Fresh and steamy apricot pies or roasts waft their flavors around the garden during the long summer days. The strength of these fragrances comes not from richness but from a soft, drug-like effect which makes everyone forget the passing of time.

This scene draws the observer into a slow, timeless world. All sensory information is natural and without discord. The scene is thus one of natural harmony, and its effect is to leave the beholder at peace.

*　　　　*

Is each essay a united whole? If it has been written in clear steps, the essay should not only be easy to follow, but it should also allow the reader to construct a plan from the paragraphs. Is this possible for each of these essays?

Look closely at the paragraphs. Are you able to identify links with the plan? Is each paragraph performing its task as an introduction, body paragraph or conclusion? How can you tell? Are you able to identify different levels of detail chosen for the various paragraphs?

Most importantly, you must ask yourself if you are satisfied that each essay has answered the question.

Now put yourself in the reader's position and carefully read over the descriptive essay you completed in exercise 5.3 ('Describe a beach scene'). Is it possible to construct a plan from the paragraphs? Is the essay a united whole? Ask other readers for their opinions and for any constructive criticisms they may have to offer.

Exercise 6.4: Drafting an essay

The essay that you have completed came from a plan drafted in exercise 5.1. One other plan was also drafted there, for the question 'Describe Santa Claus'. Draft an essay response to this question according to the steps you have been shown. Remember:

- Analyze the question

- Select relevant points
- Decide status of points

- Order points
- Make subdivisions

- Expand
- Support
- Link

- Tie together
- Sum up
- Make judgments

Now review your essay:

CHECKLIST

- Have I made clear what I'm describing?
- Have I planned for a particular angle of approach (e.g. sights, sounds, smells, rather than still things, slow things, fast things)?
- Have I been consistent in following this planned approach?
- Have I written a description rather than a narrative?
- Have I given the reader a 'weak' ending or one that makes an impact?

Descriptive

Essays for Evaluation

About This Section

This is the first of six sections containing essays written by students. The other sections deal with *narrative, discursive, expository, analytical* and *argumentative* modes of essay.

The intention of each of the 'essays for evaluation' sections is to give you a range of responses to the same question. Within this range there will be certain strengths and weaknesses which you should be able to recognize and comment on.

As you read each set of samples, see if you can place the essays in order of merit, taking into account, whether the response is relevant to the question, whether each response is logically organized; and whether the paragraphs in each essay have done their job.

Specifically, you might ask:

* Is the writer's intention clear?
* What angle of approach has been taken?
* Is this approach consistent throughout?
* Can you see any contradictions that weaken the Structure of the essay?
* Are the examples relevant?
* Is there continuity between paragraphs?
* Does the conclusion draw the threads of the essay together?
* Is the essay a united whole?

Try making your own point-form notes on each essay under the headings 'strengths' and 'weaknesses'.

Compare your impressions of these essays with those of other readers. Do they see the same strengths and weaknesses? Do they disagree with your choice of the better essays?

The descriptive essay question set for each of the three essays was: 'Describe a ski resort'.

Descriptive Essay A

The Yuppie Valley Resort is nestled into a natural hollow in the spine of a vast range. It stretches from the skyline to the valley floor. Skiers give or take away its life. By day the place is alive in every nerve; by night it is muted and still as nature reclaims her own.

At first light each building carries d heavy cloak on its shoulders, and waits stoically for spring. From the lodge and hotel windows, hundreds of expectant faces mime the same expression. In the sheds the packing machines doze, their paws and noses protruding. Beyond them, the chairlift cables haul the craggy peaks closer to the valley. From the mountain tops the Leggo town seems complete. The mountain prepares for the inevitable onslaught. Early tourists stumble from buses onto the snow with strange, labored steps. Seasoned veterans skate gracefully past them in coordinated colors. On the wider slopes, women sit down before they fall down. Wild men in football jerseys and beanies knock everyone down before being sent off. Austrian instructors survey the scene and sum up the madness with a shaking of heads.

A clear day brings the lodge-bunnies screaming, falling and slithering across the hillsides. There is no nook or cranny into which they will not fall. Nature seems to call them into every clump of trees. The mountain bears the insanity until the late afternoon, when it claims a few victims. As the sun fades, the great retreat begins.

The spidery hand of evening walks its fingers over the range and into the village, silencing the excesses of the day. Pedestrians'voices are subdued. Soon, the valley herds its guests into their burrows and order is restored. The scene settles to a winking painting, and night draws its curtain down. This popular resort is a place of contrasts, both in the physical environment and in terms of human activity. A small settlement draws huge crowds of madmen to a fast-lane sport, yet the same place is a virtual nativity scene after dark. Despite its dramatic mood swings, the valley is on everyone's list for next year.

Descriptive Essay B

If you drive to the top of a mountain, in North-East Victoria during winter, you will find a temporary piece of Europe perching on the summit. The people, buildings and the lifestyle are foreign to what we usually see in Australian resorts.

The mountain is rugged and steep. Snow covers its peak for four months of the year. Only a few areas on the summit have been developed - most is still untouched. This gives the skiers the Opportunity to ski in a more natural setting, and sightseers are able to avoid the resort completely. The resort has been well planned. All buildings are distinctly European in style with sloping roofs and no verandahs. There are no high-rise monsters here, buildings are timber and brick.

Apart from several glorious lodges, there are many restaurants and shops - also designed to suit the climate. The restaurants are warm and cozy, and smell delicious when you enter. The shops are quaint with friendly assistants to help you choose a souvenir or the right length of ski. The lifts and tows up the slopes are well placed to prevent excessive scarring to the overall picture of the resort. The slopes themselves are basically unaltered - left as they were found when the resort began.

The people you find in this resort range from city sightseers to European ski instructors who travel the world to ski all year. There are families who travel up to see and experience the snow. Then there are the people brave enough to attempt skiing. After that - the people keen enough and rich enough to be able to ski each year are able to become quite experienced. There are people of all ages and cultures in the resort. The resort appeals to all people. The ski resort is very popular as it gives Australians a taste of Europe, and Europeans feel comfortable in an environment close to their own. Above all, though, is the fact that the resort is beautiful. It lies in perfect harmony with the picturesque landscape of the mountain.

Descriptive Essay C

The Mount Terabula Ski Resort lies in a very idyllic setting, nestled in a valley. The tree-covered valley slopes down to form the snowfields, which are dotted with tiny human figures.

The resort, though artificial, lies in a perfectly natural setting. The surrounding mountains, tall and majestic, are covered with short stunted trees which are draped in snow. The mountains form a valley which creates the ski slopes the vacationers come for.

The white strips that are the skiing fields are covered with a thick carpet of snow, occasionally flecked with thick clumps of trees. Lifts decorate the scene, winding up the sides of the mountains. The slopes are also peppered with snow-loving holiday-makers.

There is a great variety of people on the slopes, from the professional skier to the novice ski-boarders. Most are attired in thick, padded, warm clothing, and all are attempting to enjoy their various sports. There is a continual flow of the eager from the resort to the slopes, and an equal flow of the tired or injured into the warm resort. The cluster of buildings that represents the resort of Terabula stands prominent. The lodge stands tall, capable of accommodating hundreds, while the office-block restaurant complex spreads across the grounds beside a variety of shops and a car-park. A trail of private and very expensive villas lies to the rear of the administration building.

Therefore, when the resort of Terabula is in such beautiful surroundings, has adequate facilities and satisfied visitors, it is indeed an idyllic setting.

Chapter 7

The Narrative Essay

A narrative essay tells a story.

Think about the difference between a description and a narration. A description paints a word-picture while a narrative advances the action. The descriptive essay on Dracula paints the different sides of his nature, but an essay that sets out to tell us about his life would be a narrative. A narrative essay does not merely give the reader information; it must have a story to tell, and it must hold the reader's interest until the end.

Generally speaking, a chronological approach is the safest way to plan a narrative essay. Imagine that you have been asked to give a narrative account of your life. A simple and logical way to plan your response would be to begin with infancy or early childhood, and then take each subsequent stage of life as it occurred in time. A chronological narrative is not your only option, but it is a simple way to structure this type of essay.

Examine the following plan of a narrative essay. Note the ways in which it is different from the descriptive form.

Example 7.1

Give a narrative account of Count Dracula's childhood.

~~found in bat cave~~

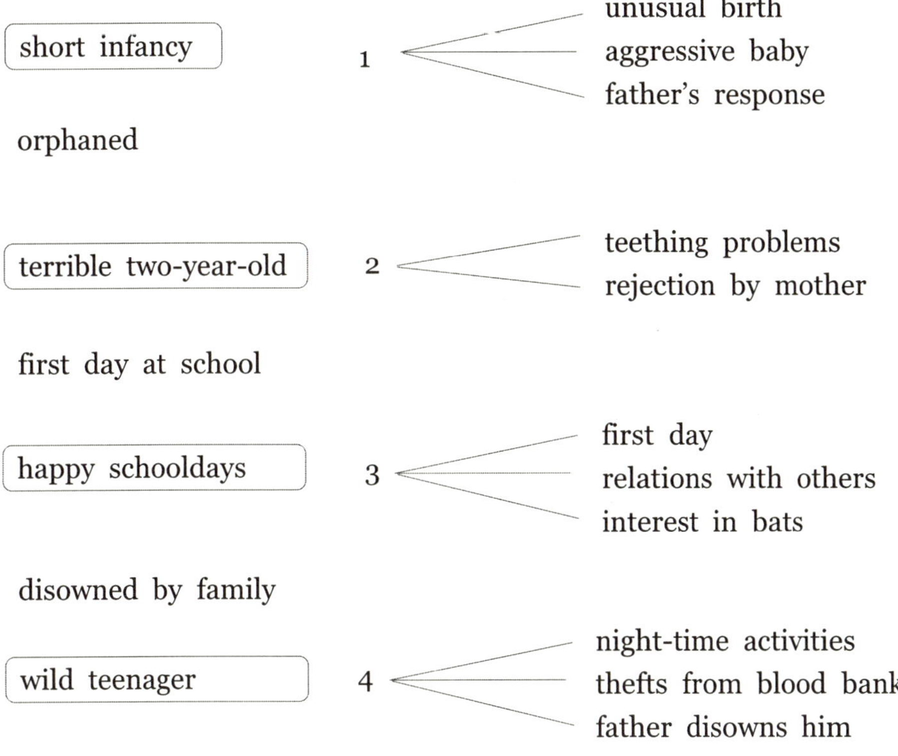

~~exile in Australia~~

This plan divides Dracula's life into stages and deals mainly with his actions and the reactions of others. The narrative is presented through a series of events. Now examine the way this plan is developed into paragraphs.

Give a narrative account of Count Dracula's Childhood.

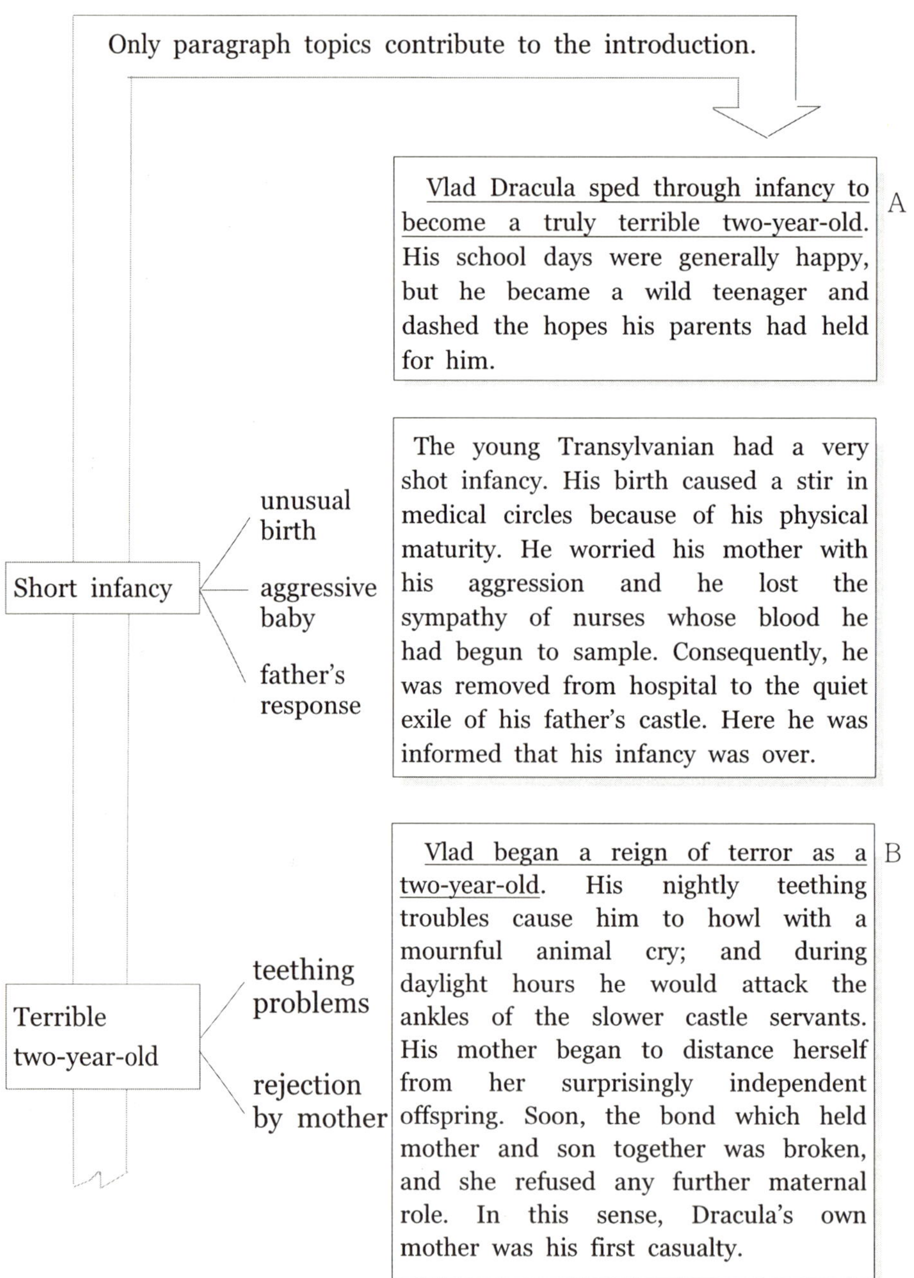

happy schooldays	first day relations with others interest in bats	Schooldays were a happy time for the boy who was unhappy at home. He was impressed, on his first day, with the innocence of the other students. He liked the way in which so many potential victims were kept in one place. As the days passed, the other students gave him a cool reception, respecting those flashing incisors. His happiest hours were those spent in nature study with his relatives, the bats. Despite his comparative isolation from other students, school was a place of great interest to Vlad, and he pleased his father with his academic success . C
Wild teenager	night-time activities thefts from blood bank Father disowns him	The Dracula family could not have prepared itself for Vlad's wild teenage years. He lived for the night-time and shunned the rest of his family. News of Vlad's activities reached his father's ears. There were sightings of mysterious bats and wolves in the neighborhood, and the blood bank in the village had been plundered repeatedly, despite tight security. Worst of all, Vlad would not account for his absences. He raged at his father when confronted with the evidence, and, each time, the father's faith in the boy ebbed away. With Vlad behaving more like a cornered animal than an aristocrat, his father formally disowned him, and Vlad's exile from the family was complete.

Childhood for Dracula proved to be an experience both hurtful and rewarding. D It was a time of frustration and rejection but also one of discovery. The great passions of his childhood were also to be the passions of his later life. Awkward relationships with his peers and his exile from the family circle foreshadowed the lonely life he would lead as an adult. E Through despised and misunderstood by many, Vlad Dracula knew, even as a child, that he would make his mark on the world.

Exercise 7.1: Planning a narrative essay

Reread the narrative account of Dracula's childhood, keeping in mind the role each paragraph is performing. Now take each underlined extract, A to E, and decide:

(1) what it does in the paragraph

(2) what it does in the essay as a whole.

This narrative essay was planned according to the same steps that you used in your descriptive essays, and that you will be using with other types of essay later. You should now have a clearer understanding of the way in which a sound plan protects the structure of the whole essay.

Exercise 7.2: Constructing a narrative essay

Your task is to construct your own narrative essay based on the question: 'Give a narrative account of your life'.

Take your time; this is a method exercise. You have a clear set of steps to follow, and you should know the importance of a carefully drafted plan.

CHECKLIST

- Have I ordered my points chronologically?
- Do my paragraphs advance the action rather than paint a picture?
- Have I told a story that is clear and logical in its presentation?
- Is my essay a united whole?

A long narrative will not necessarily be a good one. Here are a few hints that may help you to keep your reader interested:

* Draft in order to improve clarity and simplicity.
* Include only things relevant to the progress of the narrative.
* Vary paragraph openings.
* Vary the length of your sentences.
* Avoid long-winded sentences.

Additional Narrative Essay Questions

(1) Give a narrative account of the life of a Peter Pan.
(2) What happened to the people of Baekje Dynasty?
(3) Tell the story of Korea's settlement from prehistoric times to the present day.

Narrative

Essays for Evaluation

The narrative essay question set for each of the three essays was: 'Tell the story of your life.'

Narrative Essay A

My life began with an awkward birth. During infancy came the tasks of learning to walk and talk. I showed interest in surroundings at an early age. I started school at an early age and, being average academically, found it enjoyable. Adolescence was trying but filled with happy events.

I came into the world prematurely, by a Caesarian birth. There were difficulties, particularly with breathing, and allergic reactions to penicillin and to mother's milk. These first few days of my life were crucial. Most of the foods I ate then were determined by whether I reacted badly to them or not. During infancy I was sick and caught pneumonia, German measles, mumps and chicken pox, but I did not get any major illnesses, I began to walk and talk early and began to show interest in my surroundings, and was a1ways occupied. As a result, I was sent to school at the age of four. School was a lot of fun and quite enjoyable despite my average academic success. At the age of nine I changed schools and gradually settled in to my new surroundings. High school was a little frightening at first, but I soon got used to its size and the different atmosphere.

Adolescence is my most memorable stage because it is the most recent. The beginning did not happen noticeably. It was the time that I began to develop a personality of my own, and stopped being influenced by others. Because I am smaller in size than most people, I found adolescence difficult, with people not recognizing or believing my age.

Adolescence was also the time when I developed many interests, such as horse riding, skating, dancing and music. Some of these I still continue; others I have left behind. During this time, which was trying for my parents and other members of my family, I gained my own beliefs and opinions. Only a few incidents in my life stand out. These include places I have been, such as Washington, New York and Boston and people I have met, such as Bill Clinton. Other things, such as moving house and meeting relatives from England that I never knew I had, have made life enjoyable in general.

I have learned in the past few years to accept myself as I am. My friends and other people around me seem to have done the same, preferring my friendship to material things. I believe that experiencing a wide range of hobbies and interests has helped me to establish my likes and dislikes and to become the person that I am.

Narrative Essay B

My life has been quite easy, especially during my late teen years in the country. I have a good group of friends and we enjoy each other's company, even though there are some strong differences between us.

When I was seven, I fell out of Dad's car as we went round a corner. Dad had forgotten to close the door. Everyone laughed about it later, but I can still remember the wheels of trucks humming past my nose as I lay on the asphalt. Soon after this, we moved out to the country and Dad left the Tactical Response Group in Sydney for a quiet life as an explosives expert in Walla. By the time 1 was ten, I was a proper country kid.

Mother had a surprise when I was born because she thought she was expecting twins. The whole family was waiting around with two sets of everything. I was not very popular there for a while. Apparently I slept well and did not annoy people as I do now. When I was four, my father left me at school by mistake. The teachers thought it was a great joke, and gave me some work to do until I grew up. At eight years I fell off my horse and broke my leg, but my childhood was fairly uneventful otherwise.

The first time I was brought home as a baby, no one recognized me. This was not surprising because the nurses had mixed me up with the child over the road. The relatives all crowded around at first, although they soon lost interest when the real nappy work began.

Later, when I leave school, I would like to be a taxidermist or maybe a taxi driver, but for the moment I am enjoying life to the full. There have been changes which I can see have matured my character in the last year, but I still think that I was a typical Aussie child with no real hang-ups for most of my childhood. The teenage years are often considered to be the most difficult in a person's life. This was probably true for me when I was becoming interested in girls. It all turned out to be very frustrating because they pestered me in Year 6 when I certainly was not interested, but when I did make the effort in Year 9, they had all developed other interests. The lesson I learned from this stage of my life was that you should be yourself, otherwise people will see that you are only putting on a front.

Now I am in my final years of school, which have been generally happy ones. Probably the most important thing at this stage of your life is to have supportive friends, which I think I have. Looking back over my life, I see several failures and embarrassments, such as when I waited at the wrong church for Jannet's wedding, but on the whole there have been enough successes. In other words, life has been fun up to this point in time.

Narrative Essay C

Once upon a time there was a Mama and a Papa and a little baby boy. They were living a happy life on a tropical island in the middle of nowhere. Soon, along came a little baby girl. Her name was Lisa Jane. She went on to travel the world and back again, living a happy existence.

Her family was a very close-knit one. They did a lot together and were supportive. Her family consisted of her mother, a teacher, her father, also a teacher, and a brother two years older than herself. He was also born in Nauru. A brother, Shane, seven years younger than Lisa, was the only one of the children born in Australia. Lisa also had a sister, Kamala, adopted from Sri Lanka. Nine years younger than herself, Kamala was the baby of the family. Of late her pets have included a Collie dog answering to Larni, a stray cat, Nina, and a budgie, Thursday.

Lisa had traveled much in her life, having been born in Nauru. After six months she moved back to Albury, Australia. At the age of two her family moved again to Balldale, a small country town in New South Wales. This is where she 'grew up'. After the birth of her younger brother Shane, they headed off for mystical South-East Asia, where she lived with her family in Malaysia for three years. While there, they traveled to many other countries, including Thailand, Indonesia, Hong Kong, Sri Lanka, Singapore and most of Malaysia. On returning to

Australia, they moved to Albury where they have remained ever since.

Lisa has many dreams that she wishes to fulfill. Traveling to Canada later this year as an exchange student is one of these dreams. She wishes to follow a career in physiotherapy and further travel the world. Lisa, since corning into this world, has had a happy life with a caring family. She has learnt much from her travels and wishes to continue them and her education. She also wishes to learn about and help the world and its people as much as possible.

Chapter 8

The Discursive Essay

A discursive essay sets out to explore its topic by looking at it from different viewpoints, often using a 'for and against' approach.

A discussion does not take sides. The primary role of the discursive essay is to investigate the range of views relevant to its topic. You should present these views fairly, no matter what strong personal views you hold. Take the case of a computer fanatic faced with the question: 'Discuss the claim that computers do more harm than good'. He or she would be obliged to present the points for and against computers in a fair and balanced way. Although a balanced discussion does not take sides, it should still come to some conclusion at the end. At the close of the investigation, the different viewpoints may be weighed against each other, and an informed summing up made. Using the above example, the computer fanatic may have found that, on balance, computers were worthwhile.

You should plan your discursive essay by determining the balance of views at the planning stage, so that a fair exploration is made possible. It is important that you stand back from an issue and look at it from all angles. If you do allow strong personal feelings to rule your discussion, readers will not take your conclusions seriously because they will have been take on a one-sided tour of the topic.

Trace the formation of the discursive essay below. Watch for the way the plan determines the balance of viewpoints to be explored.

Example 8.1

Discuss the claim that computers do more harm than good.

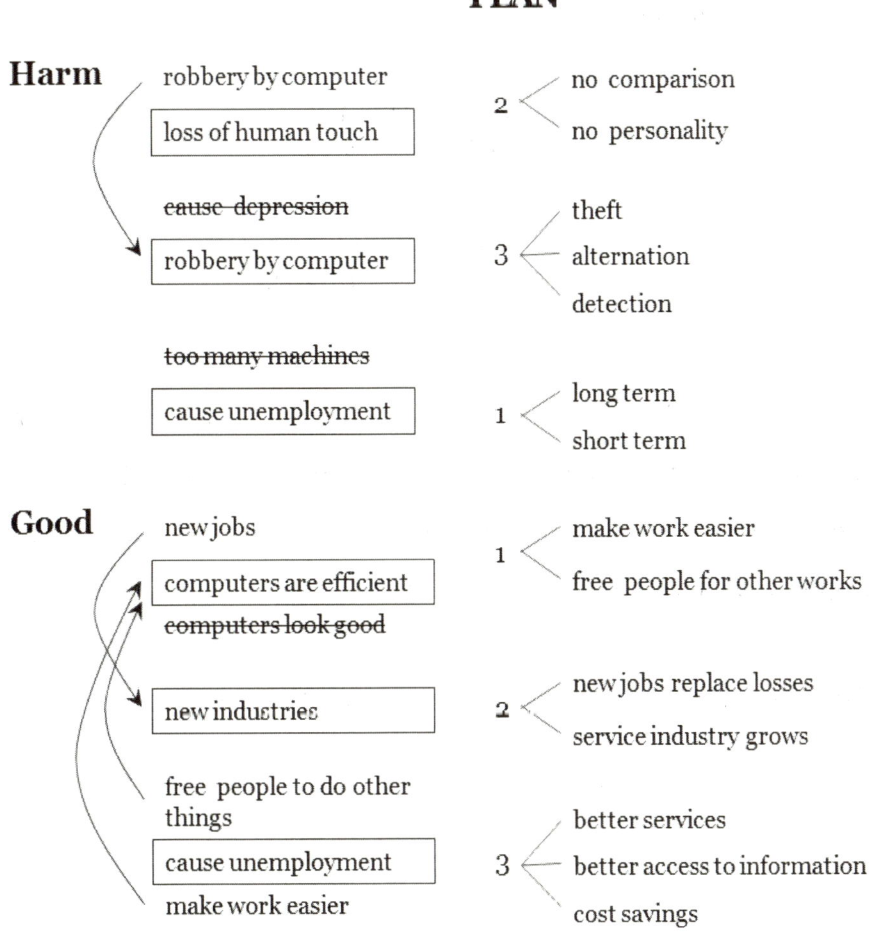

This question specifies two opposing views: 'harm' and 'good'. As equal marks will be awarded to each park, equal time has been awarded to each view. Much of the shaping of the essay has already been completed through the familiar steps:

- Analyze the question

- Select relevant points
- Decide status of points

- order points
- make subdivisions

Note that half of our operational steps are taken up with the production of the plan; the other half with writing. These first three steps will become particularly important where longer, more complicated questions are set for discussion.

Now see how the plan is used to shape the essay.

Example 8.1 (continued)

Discuss the claim that computers do more harm than good.

Paragraph topics contribute to the introduction.

Our reliance on computers has brought problems as well as benefits. Loss of employment, the impersonal nature of computers and the dangers of abuse by operators, on the one hand, must be weighed against the efficiency of the machines, the new industries created and the benefits which flow to all, on the other.

Harm

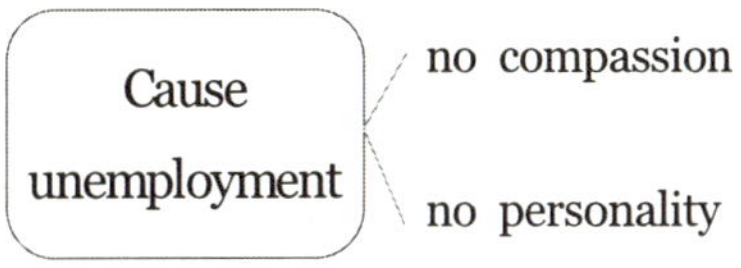

Cause unemployment

no compassion

no personality

Loss of employment opportunities has been one obvious effect of our increasing use of computers. In the short term, this can be seen in the reduced need for clerical workers, particularly in large companies. In the long term, there will be demands for operators, analysts and so on, but these are increasingly specialized jobs. While new opportunities have surfaced, the big loser has been the worker with few skills.

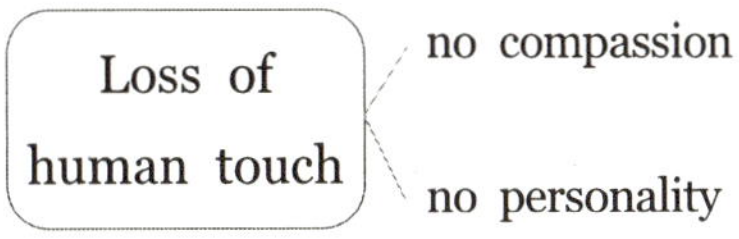

Loss of human touch

no compassion

no personality

Computers have no human touch. Machines dealing in numbers show no compassion towards people, and virtually exclude humans from most operations, especially in government departments. Although some computers have a 'voice', this is only a token form of personality. The result of this is a sterile, dehumanized workplace for employees.

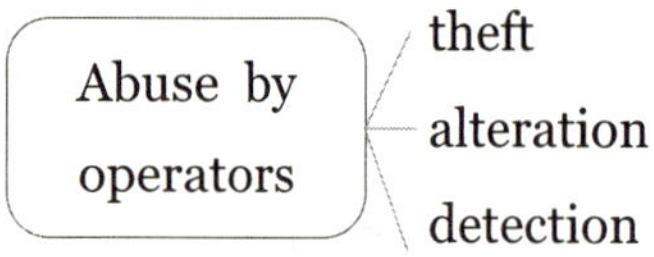

Abuse by operators

- theft
- alteration
- detection

This comment warns the reader of the importance of the point of the paragraph.

his comment links the paragraph with the question and tells the reader how important the point is.

The danger of abuse of computers by operator is a very real one. Theft of funds from large companies and banks is a major problem. Alteration of data in computerized records is another, perhaps more insidious, hazard. Detection of criminals who use such methods is made more difficult by the number of legitimate users. Illegal access by hackers is a further complication. Although companies and governments are aware of these problems and use sophisticated methods of protection and detection, the balance has not always been in their favor. The potential for criminal abuse of computers is thus a harmful aspect of their use.

Good

Computers are efficient

- make work easier
- free people for other work

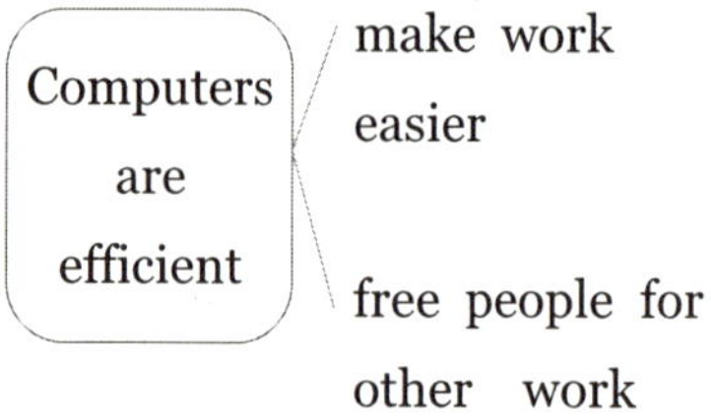

On the positive side, computers are clearly efficient. Jobs have been made easier by the elimination of many long, repetitive tasks such as the storage, retrieval and cross-referencing of information. Considerable time saving has been achieved, especially in large government departments. A significant advantage is that people released from repetitive work are free to perform in areas such as planning and decision making. Efficient computer technology has thus had important spin-off effects for the community.

new industries — new jobs replace losses; service industry grows

Computerization has spawned a wide range of new industries. Employment opportunities in retailing, software, systems analysis and services have helped replace losses caused by the use of technology. The services sector has grown substantially, particularly in the information and consultancy fields. While computers have closed some doors, they have opened others.

we all benefit — better services; better access to information; cost savings

Directly or indirectly, we all benefit from the work of computers. We are given better services by government and business. Professionals have better access to information, such as medical cases for doctors, and criminal records for police. These efficient services mean savings of time and money. On the national level, we are able to achieve more of our objectives as a result of the computer networks.

This statement prepared the reader for the summing up process.

The middle section of this conclusion summarizes the result of the discussion undertaken in the body paragraphs.

A clear judgment is made. This decision is justified by what has gone before, and answers the question.

Weighing the good against the harm done by computers, it can be seen that the technology is a double-edged sword: loss of employment in one area is balanced by growth in another; and the potential for criminal abuse is balanced by improving protection and detection. Perhaps most significantly, the computer has freed human energies for use in other areas of need. Thus, while there are drawbacks, computers clearly do more good than harm.

Exercise 8.1: Planning a discursive essay

(1) Look at the introduction of the essay given in example 8.1. Has the discussion been prejudiced or balanced at this stage? Find evidence to support your response.

(2) What can you say about the direction of the essay, having read only the introduction?

(3) Does each body paragraph deal with material specified for it in the plan? Does each one have a topic sentence and a concluding sentence?

It is important that each body paragraph is seen as one step in a whole journey, rather than as an isolated island of information. The element that best helps you to link your paragraphs is the comment or observation you make in each paragraph. These comments need not necessarily be only in the concluding sentences, but they must make links with the question and with other paragraphs.

(4) Read the conclusion of the essay. What functions are the following statements performing in the paragraph?

(a) 'it can be seen that technology is a double-edged sword'

(b) 'perhaps most significantly'

(c) 'while there are drawbacks'

(d) 'computers clearly do more good than harm'.

The question asking writers to discuss the 'good' and 'harm' done by computers is very specific. Here, the different viewpoints have been spelt out to writers. This will not always be so; the question could well have been: 'Discuss our use of computers'. In this case, the two sides of the issue are implied rather than statcd outright. Think carcfully about your qucstions, particularly the brief ones, because these often imply that certain approaches be taken. Remember why we have the step: *analyze the question.*

Exercise 8.2: Constructing a discursive essay

Your discursive essay question is: "Discuss our use of cars." The following points may be useful to you during your planning operations. Feel free to add or eliminate points in order to draft a relevant plan.

* convenience
* not restricted by schedules
* freedom
* overcome distance barrier
* allow us to visit relatives and friends more often
* fast method of travel
* comfortable
* saves us time
* cfficicnt

* relatively cheap/expensive to run
* good back-up network
* air pollution
* we can pick our favorite color in cars
* high death toll
* many injuries
* the wheels come off at high speeds
* more stressful life with cars
* faster pace of life
* we plan life around cars
* space taken for cars
* life is no longer at a human pace

Once you have drafted your plan, continue through the remaining steps to construct your essay.

CHECKLIST

- Have I determined a balance of views at the planning stage?
- Has my introduction prepared a prejudiced or balanced discussion for the reader?
- Does each body paragraph have a topic sentence and a concluding sentence?
- Have the discussion points been weighed up in the conclusion?
- After the weighing of viewpoints, have decisions been arrived at in the conclusion?

Discursive

Essays for Evaluation

*The **discursive** essay question set for each of the three essays was: 'Discuss the effects that television has had on us'.*

Discursive Essay A

There are several significant effects that television has on us, both harmful and beneficial. Some effects are obvious but others are more subtle. The benefits are that programs inform and educate us, while harmful effects can be seen in the way television can affect family life, cause addiction and present biased or misleading information.

The benefits that television brings us in the form of news and current affairs are easily demonstrated. The world is brought into our lounge rooms through the use of satellites, and we are kept up to date on developments wherever news is in the making. It must be acknowledged that there are dangers associated with this race for news: the shocking and the sensational become part of our children's television diet. It is nothing to see bodies in the streets, even on the ABC, and we become desensitized to the horrors of the world. The achievements of such an efficient service must, nonetheless, be recognized.

Other benefits include information that it is in the public's interest to know. Investigative television, such as 'Sixty Minutes' and 'The Investigators' has had an important impact on the standards which Americans set themselves. The Fitzgerald Enquiry in New York was partly the result of such television work. Despite the successes, there may be problems with televised investigation that is too intrusive, such as during high-profile court cases. A balance must therefore be found whereby both public and private interests are protected.

The educational value of television has been demonstrated through highly respected shows such as 'Sesame Street', 'Discovery Channel', 'National Geographic' and 'Living Planet'. Children's literacy and numeracy have clearly been helped by 'Sesame Street'. Television is an excellent medium through which to teach skills. The video industry has recognized this and we have benefited from this access to education which may otherwise have been unavailable. There are certainly some strong educational roles performed by television.

On the harmful side, television often dominates family life and stifles real communication. In cases where both parents work, there may be little time for the whole family to be together, and with television, conversations are usually about the shows rather than about the family. In this way television is a thief of family time.

For some people, television offers a very real chance of addiction. Soap opera shows such as 'General Hospital' and 'Days of Our Lives' may even take some viewers out of the real world, particularly where the viewers' lives are already dreary or hopeless. On a more general level, the very habit of watching television every day can have a powerful impact on the way people use their time. This is a particularly harmful and insidious effect of the medium.

Perhaps one of the greatest dangers of television is the way biased or misleading presentation of information damages people's reputations. Recent court cases have brought complaints of 'trial by media' and some current affairs presenters do set out to lead viewers by the nose. Whether viewers are being led to the truth is not always a matter of any consequence. To counter this, viewers must be prepared to use their own judgment, and must not allow themselves to be misled.

There is no doubt that television is a powerful thing; its effects on us are wide-ranging. Some of its strongest influences are also those least recognized by viewers, especially the way it moulds our opinions and steals our time. While accepting the substantial and desirable role of television in the areas of education and information, we must guard against the excesses of some presenters, and be prepared to use our judgment where theirs has failed. Television may seem to be a benevolent giant, but it is really a sly monster against which we must constantly be on our guard.

Discursive Essay B

The introduction of television to Australia forty years ago was thought to be a great advance in technology. Yet today, People are realizing that along with advantages such as enjoyment, education and a source of vital information, television also has a harmful side linked with health problems and obsession.

Noticeable health problems can result from excessive television. Instead of exercising and spending time outside in the fresh air, people become glued to the TV screen. They begin inhaling stale air and their blood does not circulate efficiently. This causes cholesterol difficulties or obesity. Thus, television can become extremely dangerous to a person's health.

Obsession is another harmful effect of television. When a person actually becomes addicted, friends and family are replaced by the TV. Eventually, human company becomes rare and the art of conversation is lost. It is also possible that people become so involved in the television world that they believe it is reality. Sometimes, they even perform violent acts to imitate their hero, while all the time thinking it is permissible. This is a very frightening aspect of television.

On the positive side, we receive a great deal of enjoyment from watching movies, comedies or a mini-series. Our minds are taken off everyday worries and we are allowed to relax. Becoming involved in the fantasy world is an excellent way to unwind and make ourselves at ease.

Television is also a reliable source of information as we are told of world-wide current affairs, either disasters or fortunate occurrences. Such things as sport, weather predictions and advertisements are broadcast, allowing us to keep up to date with the latest events.

Knowledge is also gained from television. Educational programs like 'Play School'and 'Sesame Street' teach children as well as provide entertainment, whilst documentaries help educate adults in serious matters. Therefore society benefits from this.

Looking at the good and the harmful side of television, we should be able to see that, when used wisely, it is very advantageous. So, while there are disadvantages, it is clear that television is more beneficial than harmful to us.

Discursive Essay C

The effect that television has on people in today's society is enormous. Not only does it affect us mentally, but physically as well. In this essay, I will attempt to discuss the good points as well as the obvious problems associated with television.

Television is one of the most remarkable inventions made this century, and is a very important part of our lives. Although generations before us have lived quite well without television, today's society would be far from what it is now without it.

Firstly, education would be different. Schools would not have video resources and young children would not be able to watch the various children's shows now available to help them learn and understand.

Television should be used as a way to relax and relieve tension and stress. But, in general, people these days have grown lazier since television has been introduced into the home. People are now able to sit and watch the wide variety of television shows available, instead of being outside getting sufficient exercise. Because of this, growing weight problems have occurred as well as, for some people, lack of sleep, which is also unhealthy.

If not for the television and its industry, many people working as actors, directors, script writers and camera men, just to name a few, would not be in that line of work. Therefore if television was not around, maybe the unemployment statistics would be sky-high! These actors also have a strong influence on various people who devotedly follow their favorite stars' lives each episode of the soap operas. Many television shows have been blamed for the suicides and murders of young people recently. People who get so involved in movies and television and relate them back to real life can be affected mentally, and in some cases people do become violent. This is obviously a problem, but not a major everyday problem.

When we look back and review the effect that television has had on us, we see that it is a practical part of our lives. It provides us with entertainment and enjoyment and although it has minor drawbacks, it is an appliance that we cannot live without.

* * *

Each of the three essay types examined so far gives the topic as a starting point but few guidelines are given. This allows you the freedom to be creative, imaginative and to explore ideas.

The next three types of essay, *expository, analytical* and *argumentative*, usually involve specified material and a particular task is given. These essays require a logical and thoughtful response.

The three steps, of question analysis, planning and writing apply to all three types, but there is further work required where a *source* is involved.

Before planning the essay you should:

* make sure you understand the source material
* be able to summarize what was said
* work out the importance of ideas presented and the strength of the evidence used to support them.

Chapter 9

The Expository Essay

An expository essay sets out to explain something to the reader. Its main purpose is to increase the reader's understanding of the topic.

An expository essay may explain, for instance, how something works, what conditions existed at a particular time in history or how something is done.

Before you can begin to explain something to the reader, you must have a sound knowledge of your material and know exactly what you aim to explain.

The ordering of this material and the clarity of your explanation are crucial elements in this type of essay. Too often, students assume that the reader will always follow and understand. This is not necessarily the case; it is up to you to prepare the reader's path.

It may be useful to assume that the reader knows nothing

about the topic. This will help you to think carefully about your choice of technical terms and about the amount of detail you are asking the reader to take in.

Only information that is essential to your explanation should be included. This is a difficult area for many writers. The word 'essential'should be kept in mind when you are choosing which material to include in your essay and which you should leave out.

There should be a logical sequencing of information. You should decide on the sequence at the planning stage.

Finally, the expository essay should be drafted where time permits.

Summary

1. Know your material.
2. Know what you are trying to explain
3. Assume that the reader knows nothing about the topic.
4. Plan your information in a logical order.
5. Eliminate any information not essential to your explanation
6. Draft your essay where time permits.

Example 9.1

What was it like in the bush during the Depression of the 1930s?

Paragraph Topics	Examples
Meaning of Depression	sustained economic collapse little commercial activity severe unemployment
Dole Income Stresses	debt problems unemployment dole barter, rabbits, wood
~~Depression in cities~~ Problems for big families	size costs health problems overcrowding scarce resources
Limited range of foods	salted meals bread dripping, golden, syrup, jam
Old clothes	lack of shoes, underwear patched hand-me-downs nothing new
radio Simple entertainments	radio where available singing at piano country show, picture show playing with matches

This question is an open one. It is up to the writer to decide what subject matter is worthy of inclusion. The plan shows two levels of detail: paragraph topics and examples. However, there is room for further subdivision. For example, 'debt problems' and 'health problems' are more general than 'lack of shoes' and 'singing at piano'. On the other hand, a high degree of specific comment on each topic is not required because the question really asks for a general impression of conditions. When planning an answer to such a question, you must keep the overall picture in mind: what it was like and which main topics deserve coverage. At the same time, you should include enough specific detail to support your points and satisfy the reader's interest. Finally, you must test the plan against the terms of the question.

Now read the completed essay.

What was it like in the bush during the Depression of the 1930s?

The Great Depression was a period of sustained economic collapse. For most Australians, this meant little commercial activity and severe unemployment. The Depression had a deep impact on all people in the bush, although it affected some families more dramatically than others. There were major pressures on the types of entertainment that were available.

Considerable pressures were brought to bear on families, particularly the larger ones. Those struggling to keep ten or more children faced a limited food supply and the danger of killer diseases such as diphtheria and gastro-enteritis. A lack of resources such as bedding commonly resulted in wheat bags being used for blankets by children. The results of poverty and overcrowding may be partly measured in the number of deaths amongst children.

Stresses on the incomes of bush families varied according to ownership of land and to the degree of indebtedness. The combination of debt and unemployment forced many farming families from their land, after which the dole was the only choice for many. Bartering goods, for instance grain for flour, was one option for some. Other income was sought from the sale of rabbit skins and wood. The constant uncertainty and threat of poverty proved a great frustration for the larger families in the bush.

Limited incomes meant that the range of foods available was also limited. The lack of proper refrigeration frequently meant that any affordable meats had to be salted. Families under stress relied on home-made bread, jam, dripping or perhaps golden syrup or honey. Probably the strongest feature of bush food at this time was its monotony.

Clothing problems, especially for children in battling families, were keenly felt. Patched hand-me-downs were common, and younger children often had to go without shoes. Some items, such as underwear, became luxuries that only the elder children of struggling families could even hope to have. It was the children who often bore the brunt of the clothing crisis.

Bush entertainments were simple in the depressed early 1930s. Radios were becoming available for those who could afford them, but most entertainments required payment, which precluded the involvement of big families. For children from battling households, the country show was a time to window shop rather than spend. Town picture shows were fine if you could sneak in as a youngster. Around the home, adults sang around a piano where possible. Unlike today, bush entertainments revolved around the involvement of the whole family.

The Depression years in the bush were certainly stressful for many, and brought adult pressures to bear on children in large families. The uncertainty of incomes and the crisis of indebtedness loomed ominously over households. Despite the bleak outlook, simple pleasures were enjoyed and a hardy resourcefulness evolved in the growing children soon to face World War II.

One of the most common problems for the expository writer is the poor sequencing of information. Suppose you were asked to explain how to drive a manual car. If you launched into the operation of the controls before explaining the function of those controls, you would confuse rather than inform the reader. A more logical ordering of paragraphs in the planning stage would help rectify this problem.

Even where paragraph order has been carefully prepared, the way information is presented *within paragraphs* is still very important. Clear and simple topic sentences are vital, especially where detailed or complex material is to be explained. If you had to explain how to drive a manual car, how would you explain the role of the brakes or the instrument panel? On a more difficult level, how would you describe the function of the gears? Compare your explanations with those of other students and listen, to their comments. If you assume that the reader knows nothing of the topic, this should remind you to keep your topic sentences simple.

Do not wait for an essay question in order to practice your skills of exposition. Try drafting expository paragraphs that explain everyday items to an audience not familiar with them. 'Test-drive' these explanations on other readers or, later, re-read them yourself. Remember to listen to the advice of other readers where possible, and be prepared to make changes for the sake of clarity.

Exercise 9.1: Planning an expository essay

This first exercise only requires plans for each expository question. Take the time to draft each plan carefully so that logic and clarity are preserved.

(1) Explain *either* (a) the greenhouse effect *or* (b) how a democratic government works

(2) Explain *either* (a) how a bicycle works *or* (b) the conditions under which convicts lived in the early years of the penal settlement at Sydney.

Examine your plans, paying close attention to the sequence of information in each case. Does each plan provide a clear and logical explanation?

Exercise 9.2: Constructing an expository essay

This question requires you to draft both the plan and the essay.

* Explain *either* (a) the role of a police force in a democracy *or* (b) the role of Prosecutors' Office in Korean politics and the presidential election.

CHECKLIST

- Did I understand clearly what I had to explain?
- Did I assume that the reader knows nothing of the topic?
- Did I plan for a logical sequencing of information?
- Are my topic sentences clear and simple?
- Where possible, have other readers tested my explanation?

Additional Expository Essay Questions

(1) What functions do the corrective services perform in Korea?

(2) Explain how to operate a motor cycle.

(3) Explain why the earth's ozone is at risk, and why we should be particularly wary of the dangers.

Expository

Essays for Evaluation

The expository essay questions set for each of the three essays was: 'Explain how to drive a manual car'.

Expository Essay A

To drive a manual automobile, you must understand the many procedures involved. I will explain to you how to start the vehicle, then how to take off, change gears, use your indicators, turn corners and, finally, I will show you how to stop your vehicle safely.

After we have entered the vehicle and we feel comfortable, it is time to start the automobile. To do so, we must place the gearshift into first (refer to top of gear knob on gearshift). When doing this, the clutch must be in. After putting it in gear we must then press in the clutch again and start the vehicle using the key. (Be careful not to rev the motor too much.) After this has been done, we may start our drive.

To Start our drive we must slowly release the clutch while slowly pressing the accelerator in. (Be sure to keep the revs at a steady pace.) When you have completely released your foot from the clutch you may then keep pressing the accelerator to gain more speed.

When the revs reach a high level (about four to five thousand revs per minute) it is then time to change into a higher gear. To do so, we must push in the clutch and let the accelerator out. It is then time to move the gearshift into second gear (refer to the gearshift knob). When the gearshift has been placed into second, we may then release the clutch while pressing in the accelerator; this procedure is used for changing both up and down gears.

Now that we feel comfortable with the gears, it is time to attempt the corner. As we approach the corner we must use our indicators to signal to other drivers which way we are going. After doing this we must then start to slow down and change into a lower gear (second or third). This will enable us to take the corner with complete control. When we reach the corner we can safely turn.

Now that we have taken the corner safely and completed most of our obstacles, it is time to pull over to the side of the road. To do this safely, we use our indicators and slow down, using both the brake and the clutch. The use of the clutch here prevents the car from stalling. When we are completely stopped on the side of the road, we may turn the engine off using the key. We may then remove our feet from the pedals.

Driving a manual car will become an everyday thing once you get used to the gears, indicators, road rules, taking off and pulling up. These procedures will become second nature after a little practice. The only thing you need to become a safe driver is control of your car at all times. All these things put together will make your driving experience a whole lot easier.

Expository Essay B

Driving a car involves an understanding of many points. To be a competent driver, you must understand the rules of the road and car maintenance as well as how the car operates. It is important to tackle every aspect of driving before getting behind the wheel. Although the layout of automobiles differs with each model, the position of the essentials is similar. From the driver's seat, the steering wheel is in front. The gear change is either on the Boor by your left hand, in which case it is called a floor shift, or on the left-hand side of the wheel, which is called a column shift.

Pedals on a car are the same on all manuals. From left to right, they are: clutch, brake and accelerator. The clutch disengages the engine from the wheels. Brakes are on all four wheels to slow or stop the vehicle's motion. The accelerator governs the revs of the motor.

The hand-brake is located either between the seats or under the steering column. The gears on an automobile enable the vehicle to tackle different gradients whilst maintaining a rev speed comfortable to the engine. There are usually four forward gears and one reverse. First is used when going from a standstill. Second is the follow-on, or for steep hills. Third is the next in sequence, then fourth, the cruising gear. Refer to the diagram on the gear stick for the position of gears. When changing gears, listen to the engine pitch; when it is high, change up to the next gear. Change by depressing the clutch with your left foot and let off some accelerator with your right. Engage the next gear. Now let the clutch off whilst pushing the accelerator. The same sequence applies to changing down through the gears.

The lights are located on a panel under the wheel. They have a high beam (used in dark conditions where there are no other cars around) and a low beam (used in traffic). The indicators are behind the wheel and move on a stick. The horn is on the wheel. Wipers are on a binnacle near the indicators.

Dials or readouts on a car include the speedometer, (giving velocity in km/h), the odometer (giving total distance traveled), the tachometer (giving revs per minute), the temperature gauge and the petrol gauge.

The most important thing to remember on the road is to obey the rules. Road rules may be found in the Motor Transport Authority booklet, but in all cases you should obey the signs and pointers around you.

Many car owners have experienced the problem of their cars not starting. For all mechanical problems you should call your roadside repairer or emergency road services. They will endeavor to remedy any problems you have. Bigger problems are usually referred to a mechanic.

When buying a second-hand car, always look for the obvious signs of deterioration. The car should have a bill-of-sales slip, a certificate of proof that the car is roadworthy. Even so, the car should be test-driven so that you can get the feel of it.

Now you should have grasped the fundamentals of driving and should be on your way to becoming a competent driver. Never become careless, and keep all your skills in good practice. This way you will stay a good and safe user of our roads.

Expository Essay C

Driving a manual car is complicated at first, but can become easier as your knowledge of methods, laws, instruments and controls increases. There are many basic things which must be considered all at once while driving: a knowledge of the car's instruments and the laws and methods vital to safe driving.

One of the main considerations of driving a manual car concerns these basic things. First you need a manual car, a driver, a place to drive, and some knowledge of the controls, laws and instruments. You must have these things if a manual car is to be driven successfully. Therefore, a learner's first considerations are these basic needs.

Because there are so many instruments and controls in a manual car, a knowledge of where they are and how they help is essential. They can be divided up into four groups: safety equipment, foot controls, hand controls and gauges. Safety equipment, made for the driver's safety, can be found everywhere on the car. Seat belts are connected just behind the seats, and the hand-brake can be found under the dash or on the floor on either side of the driver's seat. There is more safety equipment that is not really necessary for actual driving. The foot controls can be found on the floor of the car. These include, from left to right: clutch pedal, brake pedal and accelerator. As expected, all hand controls are within arm's reach on the dash or by the sides of the seat. The most important are the steering wheel, on the dash, the gear stick, usually on the floor, and switches for various things, which are found on the dash. All gauges are found on the dash in front of the driver.

When you know where all the controls are, you should learn what each one does and what it is used for. The safety equipment is built for the passengers' and the car's safety. The seat belts restrain the passengers from going through the windscreen, and locks protect the car against theft. The clutch is used to disengage the motor while stopping and changing gears. The brake and accelerator are used for stopping, and controlling the motor's running speed. There are various hand controls, but the most important are the steering wheel (used to steer the car), the gear stick (used to change gears), and switches, such as the indicator switch which is used to warn other drivers that the car will be turning. The gauges show the driver what is happening in the car and warn the driver about any faults which the car may have.

When a knowledge of the car's controls has been gained, it is then possible for the learner driver to actually begin to drive. The first thing to do is to hop in, buckle up the seat belt and check some of the safety equipment such as the rear view mirrors on the windscreen and on the doors. Then, start the car after making sure that it is in neutral gear. Then, by depressing the left-most pedal, the clutch, disengage the motor and select the desired gear, either first or reverse. First must always be selected when taking off or going very slowly, in order to use the engine's power most efficiently. Then, as the car speeds up, the next highest gear is selected. These gears can be engaged by moving the gear stick to a certain position for each gear.

A label can be found either on the gear stick or near it, showing the various gears and their positions. Once the required gear is found, the clutch must be let out to engage the motor. However, if the motor's speed varies greatly from the wheel speed, then the clutch must be let out slowly while 'revs' are applied with the accelerator. This happens when taking off. The driver should carefully listen to the motor at all times. If it sounds too high or low, then a more appropriate gear should be chosen. The steering wheel is used at all times by the driver to steer. To slow down, the driver can either slowly work down through the gears or apply the clutch pedal and press lightly on the brake.

There are many laws and methods that drivers must follow while driving on public roads for safety's sake. Some road rules have been made to protect the public and the driver. For example, you must indicate before turning and restricting your speed and a driver who is found disobeying these rules will be penalized. Some complications involved in the driving of a manual car cannot be totally avoided. Almost all cars can break down and overheat. Therefore, it is best to have such things as spare tires and jacks, and insurance against accidents is recommended.

Driving a car is quite complicated, but can be made easier by learning all the road rules and the controls of a manual car. Because a knowledge of laws, controls and requirements plays such an important role in the driving of a manual car, these things must all be accounted for when you learn to drive. If all of these rules are followed and considerations taken into account, the driving of a manual car can be both easy and safe. Unfortunately, complications such as breakdowns and tire blowouts cannot be avoided by the most aware and careful driver, so it is best to be prepared as well.

Chapter 10

The Analytical Essay

The analytical essay separates its topic into parts in order to examine and understand it more fully.

It is important that you understand the requirements of the analytical essay. Firstly, you should separate the topic into its component parts just as a mechanic would do when analyzing a mechanical problem. Secondly, each main part must be examined and its contribution to the whole must be determined (e.g., the role of the sparkplug in a misfiring engine). Finally, there must be some clear understanding of the whole based on the analysis of the parts (e.g., the relative importance of different parts of the engine as contributors to the misfiring problem).

Summary

1. Decide on the main elements to be analyzed.
2. Determine the characteristics of each element and the effect of each on the problem.
3. Combine the findings on each element examined. What understanding of the whole problem has been gained?

An analytical question may not always present a problem. For example, 'Analyze the role of police in Australia'presents an issue rather than a problem. One of the dangers you face in answering this type of question, is substituting mere description for analysis. You must avoid this *in the plan.*

A plan for this question might include paragraph topics such as 'enforcing laws', 'maintaining order' and 'investigating crimes'. However, these would only lead to a description unless the plan also indicated, for instance, how successfully each role is performed. In other words, *an analytical plan should combine paragraph topics with point-form critical comment.*

Example 10.1

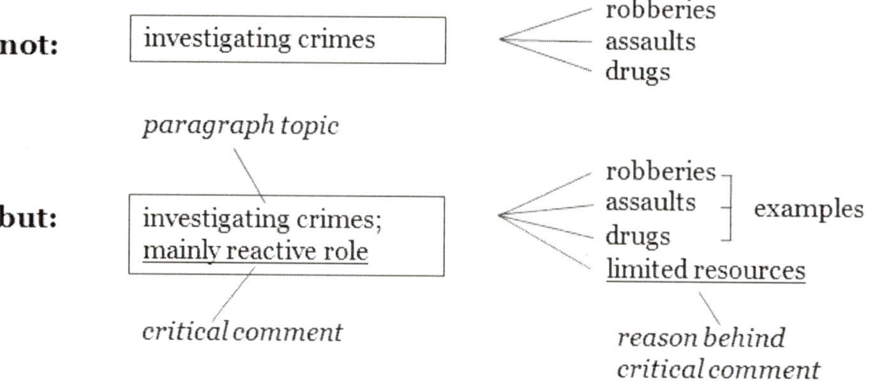

Now look at example 10.2 on the following page. It shows how all the steps of analysis are applied to the topic 'Analyze the misfiring problem in this motor'.

Example 10.2

Analyze the misfiring problem in this motor.

STEPS	POINTS	PARAGRAPHS
DECIDE THE MAIN ELEMENTS TO BE ANALYSED	gears → electrical system spark plug ~~clutch~~ fuel system lubrication	Several aspects of this motor must be analyzed if the fault is to be understood. The electrical system, the fuel system and the lubrication of the motor are the elements requiring close study.
DETERMINE THE CHARACTERISTICS OF EACH ELEMENT AND THE EFFECT OF EACH ON THE PROBLEM OR ISSUE	Electrical leads not conducting well → an unreliable element of this motor sparkplug dirty, corroded → definitely one cause of misfiring lubrication operating smoothly → poses no threat to operation of motor fuel tank dirty, lines partly blocked → contributing factor to erratic firing of sparkplug	The electrical leads prove to be poor conductors of current. This is an unreliable element in the motor. The dirty and corroded sparkplug is definitely one cause of misfiring, and adds to the lack of reliability. Lubrication of the motor is operating smoothly. Moving parts are not in any danger from excessive friction of heat. This element poses no threat to the operation of motor. The fuel system has two problems. Firstly, the tank is dirty and is thus a source of contamination. Secondly, the fuel lines are partly blocked. Both elements of the fuel supply contribute to the erratic firing of the sparkplug.
COMBINE THE FINDINGS ON EACH ELEMENT EXAMINED. WHAT UNDERSTANDING OF THE WHOLE PROBLEM OR ISSU HAS BEEN GAINED?	a combined of factors contributes to loss to reliability lubrication not a factor both parts of the fuel supply contribute to the problem electrical system, especially sparkplug, contributes to the problem	The motor misfires because of a combination of factors, each of which contributes to a loss of reliability. Although lubrication was not a factor, both parts of the fuel supply, the electrical system and the sparkplug in particular are combined to cause the misfiring problem.

Exercise 10.1: Planning an analytical essay

Now it is time for you to try your hand at analysis. This first exercise requires only a plan in response to each question. Take the time to draft plans that will combine paragraph topics with critical comment.

(1) Analyze the role of police in Korea.
(2) Analyze the impact of pollution on the earth.

Examine both plans closely. Is each one analytical rather than descriptive?

Exercise 10.2: Constructing an analytical essay

This exercise requires you to draft both the plan and the essay.
* Analyze the impact television has had on the lives of Koreans.

CHECKLIST

- Have I decided the main elements to be analyzed?
- Have I made critical comment on each of these?
- Have I considered my findings and made broader comment on the whole?
- Is my response concerned with analysis rather than description?

Analytical

Essays for Evaluation

The analytical essay question set for each of the three essays was: 'Analyze the role of the police in Australia'.

Analytical Essay A

The police in Australia have several roles in the community, which are carried out with varying degrees of success. The main roles of the police force are to protect life and property, to enforce laws introduced by governments, to deter would-be criminals and to solve crimes.

The primary role of any police force should be to protect life and property. In this country, this aim has been achieved to a high degree in most areas. However, because of vast distances, some remote communities are left to protect themselves. This role of the police is vital to members of society who are vulnerable and unable to protect themselves, for example the very young and the very old. Lack of manpower in larger cities has often made this goal difficult to achieve, but the police have generally been successful.

Enforcing laws introduced by parliamentarians is another role for the police. Enforcing some laws may over-ride the need to enforce others. The recent case of the rebel egg farmer who did not conform to the appropriate laws and was evicted and had his chickens slaughtered illustrates the way the animal protection laws may be over-ridden. Enforcing the laws of parliaments is a role that is performed effectively by police, although police numbers determine that a priority system must be applied to requests for police help.

Solving crimes and convicting lawbreakers is an important aspect of police work. Success in this area has improved dramatically in recent years with the help of modern technology, such as forensic evidence and computerized records. Despite these advantages, the sharp increase in drug-related crimes has placed a heavy burden on police resources and manpower. Most metropolitan police forces have agreed that drug-related crimes are by far the biggest threat in today's society. A New South Wales police commissioner said recently that they were fighting a losing battle against organized crime and drugs, and predicted that the situation would not improve until adequate funding was allocated to the police force.

Crimes committed also include those done by police. Recent revelations from the Fitzgerald Enquiry have demonstrated that police corruption, at all levels of the force, can have a devastating effect on the effectiveness and the morale of a state's police force. Similar problems in New South Wales and other states suggest that corruption is causing a significant loss of effectiveness in many areas of police activity. As a result of this, the public perception of police forces may have become more negative.

Today, police forces in Australia generally maintain a satisfactory level of law and order. The protection of life and property and the enforcement of most laws are carried out with competence and authority. However, in today's society, the police are facing an increasing occurrence of organized crime, from within and without, and unless governments act accordingly with funding and manpower, the situation will deteriorate.

Analytical Essay B

To analyze the role of police in Australia we must establish some individual roles that police take on, such as security and protection the very important police rescue, the setting of an example on and off duty, and the encouragement of community involvement in police work.

Security and protection are generally the most common police roles that provide safety in Australia. Random breath testing is very well done in the eastern states, considering the lack of manpower. All over Australia, highway patrolling is executed with professionalism. Foot patrols are not as good as they could be; the main problem is the lack of manpower. Overall, security and protection are good.

The setting of an example to the public by police is lacking, as seen by the events of the Fitzgerald Enquiry in Queensland. The enquiry involved political and police corruption. Police behavior in public is somewhere between fair and good, taking into account violence, corruption, and the few police in Australia who are involved in organized crime, especially in Queensland.

Police rescue is one of the more pleasing aspects of effective police work. Helicopter rescue is a lifesaving service. The Victorian Police use Medivac Helicopters, an example which other states are now following Water rescue is very well conducted too. Many lives have been saved on the water when the sailors would otherwise have drowned.

Community involvement is attempted nationwide. Neighborhood Watch is a program that encourages people to tell police if a crime is expected to be committed in a local neighborhood. This has proved to be very efficient in stopping burglaries. Operation Noah is held a few times a year; it is the public's chance to tell police of any drug-related offences being committed.

'Crime Stoppers' is a nationwide television program which re-enacts crimes that have been committed. Because of the program, several escapees and murderers have been caught, which proves the show to be worthwhile. The involvement of the community in police work is proving to be worthwhile.

Overall, police work in Australia is done well, especially police rescue, community involvement and security and protection. The setting of an example to the public is two-sided, with corruption in Queensland letting the side down.

Analytical Essay C

The role of police in Australia covers several areas. Enforcing the law, finding and dealing with offenders, protecting people and maintaining order are the areas covered by police in Australia. They cover some of these areas better than others.

The major role of police in Australia is to enforce the law. The law can be broken up into two parts: criminal law and civil law. It is the role of police to enforce both parts of the law. Criminal law involves protecting the community from people who violate the safety and the interest of its members. Civil law deals with the rights of individuals, and aims to ensure that the individual is given protection from people who may wish to interfere with their rights. In both these areas the police do their best to uphold and enforce the law. However, criminal activity still occurs and some people have their rights infringed upon.

Finding and dealing with offenders against the law involves a number of things. Firstly, a crime must be investigated to discover the offender. After this, the offender is apprehended and arrested. Both these aspects are done well, considering they are not easy jobs. Last of all, the offender must be dealt with or punished in some wav. This usually means a court hearing where a judge hands down a sentence. The police must deal with all these areas, although in the last area it is not often the police who deal with punishing offenders.

Another responsibility of the police is to protect people. In this, they try to prevent accidents and unnecessary deaths, although both of these are becoming more frequent. They also try to prevent criminal activity so that people, and their belongings, are kept from danger. This aspect, however, like the previous aspect, has not been dealt with completely successfully as crimes are constantly being committed. Protecting people is an extremely difficult task for the police to perform.

Maintaining order in society involves preventing riots and upholding a level of fairness and justice. Preventing riots eliminates some unnecessary violence and provides, to some extent, peace within a community. This is done rather well by police in Australia. Upholding a level of fairness and justice also helps maintain order. By preserving the status quo the people are kept content, knowing that in all circumstances they will be treated correctly and on a par with other people. The police also do this quite well, although not everyone feels that he or she is treated fairly.

The role of police in Australia covers a wide range of activities and responsibilities, and although some of these responsibilities are not performed as well as others, they are all carried out to a certain extent. Enforcing the law, finding and dealing with offenders, protecting people and maintaining order all combine to form the role of police in Australia.

Chapter 11

The Argumentative Essay

An argumentative essay sets out to persuade the reader to hold a particular view by taking him or her through a series of reasoned steps to a logical conclusion.

A clear, persuasive argument has several important structural features. Firstly, it *defines* the key terms in the question. For instance, in the question 'Is random breath testing necessary for Australians?', the term 'random breath testing' would need to be given a specific meaning at the outset.

Secondly, it makes a short statement that sums up the case to be presented to readers; for instance 'random breath testing is necessary because it saves lives'. This statement is called a *contention* or *line of argument.*

Thirdly, the contention is *developed* and *supported* through steps that are reasonable and accessible to readers. The contention 'breath testing saves lives' could be developed through paragraph topics such as 'effect of alcohol on drivers' 'alcohol and road deaths', 'innocent victims' and so on. Within each of these paragraphs, relevant supporting evidence is offered. In this case, evidence could include specific effects of alcohol on drivers, comparative statistics on road deaths and the specific types of innocent victims at risk. A further task may be required in this part of the essay; this is the *countering* or *rebuttal* of other arguments opposing your own.

Finally, a persuasive argument must end with a logical conclusion – a judgment that it is now reasonable to make. In this example, a reasonable concluding statement could be: 'Random breath testing combats alcohol abuse by drivers and saves innocent lives, so it is essential that we have it'.

Summary

1. Define key terms in the question.
2. State your contention or main line of argument
3. Develop your contention through body paragraph topics; support it with relevant examples. During this stage it may be necessary to rebut counter-arguments
4. State the conclusions or judgments at which readers should logically arrive.

Refer to Example 10.1, and follow each of the stages as the argument in favor of random breath testing is developed.

How soon did you have a clear idea of what would be argued? Did you find that the steps you followed were reasonable? Were the examples relevant to the case? Was the conclusion linked to the rest of the essay?

Arguments pose several problems for students. Surprisingly, many students do not tell readers what is to be argued at the outset. It is not good enough that the readers assume or guess your contention after, reading half the essay. Make a bold statement at the start.

A second area of concern is that some writers argue both sides of a case, leaving the readers to make their own decisions at the end. This would be discussion rather than argument. Keep in mind that an argumentative essay requires you to argue the case for a particular point of view. You cannot 'sit on the fence'.

Thirdly, it is important that you do not ask the reader to make jumps in logic. When you link your evidence and comments to conclusions, the progression must seem to be a *reasonable* one. For example, it is reasonable to say that passengers, riders, drivers and pedestrians are put at risk by drunken drivers, and that random breath testing would help protect them. It is unreasonable to say that all passengers should be tested. There are texts that examine errors of logic; you may wish to read relevant books and materials.

Summary

1. Do say what you will argue at the start of the essay.
2. Do develop your case in reasonable steps.
3. Do make conclusions that are supported by your evidence.
4. Do not sit on the fence.
5. Do not make sweeping, unsupported statements.
6. Do not make the reader jump in order to reach your conclusions.

Exercise 11.1: Planning an argumentative essay

Here are two questions that have caused considerable debate in Korea. Drafting only a plan in each case, prepare arguments for them.

(1) Should the meat with bones from the U.S.A. be imported to Korea?
(2) State the case for the abolition of capital punishment.

Examine both plans closely. Does each have a clear contention or main reason? Is each paragraph topic relevant to the contention? Are the examples directly supportive of the paragraph topics? What conclusions would it be reasonable to reach, given the material in each plan?

Example 11.1

Is random breath testing necessary for Australians?

STEPS	PLAN	PARAGRAPHS
DEFINE TERMS	random breath testing is: breath analysis of the blood-alcohol levels of motorists at police discretion	Random breath testing is the measurement of the blood-alcohol levels of motorists through breath samples taken at the discretion of the police. This testing is a simple, effective and necessary method of saving lives on our roads.
STATE YOUR CONTENTION	random breath testing saves lives	
DEVELOP YOUR CONTENTION THROUGH BODY PARAGRAPH TOPICS AND SUPPORT AT STRATEGIC POINTS WITH RELEVANT EXAMPLES	effect of alcohol on drivers — socially accepted drug; causes drowsiness, impairs judgment, affects co-ordination and reaction time (2006 figures)	Alcohol is a socially acceptable drug in Australia. As a depressant it can seriously affect drivers through drowsiness and impaired judgment, and through poor co-ordination and reaction time. In 2005 thirty-two percent of Australian road accidents were related to alcohol. The dangers of alcohol for Australian drivers are clear.
	alcohol and road deaths — NSW figures on deaths: before and after random breath resting	Many road deaths can be directly attributed to alcohol abuse. In New South Wales random breath testing has dramatically reduced fatalities from 653, January to June 1982, to 468 for the same period, 1983. Since its introduction preventative random breath testing reduced road accidents and fatalities more than successfully.
	Innocent victims — passengers; drivers; riders; pedestrians	Innocent people are in danger from drivers influenced by alcohol. Innocent drivers, passengers, riders and pedestrians, particularly the very old and the very young, are put at risk by drunken drivers. Random breath testing helps provide vital protection for these people, as s their right.
	Random breath testing and road laws — seat belt laws; speeding laws	Road laws are intended to promote safety, as are laws governing random breath test. Each serves a protective function by reducing injury and death. Random breath testing should therefore be an important component of road laws for all states.
STATE THE CONCLUSIONS THAT YOU WISH READERS TO REACH	* random breath testing combats alcohol abuse * it protects innocent people * it reinforces road laws	In order to combat alcohol abuse by drivers, to reduce the loss of innocent lives and to make our road laws work for us, we must have random breath testing. Our lives may depend on it.

Is random breath testing necessary for Australians?

Random breath testing is the measurement of the blood-alcohol levels of motorists through breath samples taken at the discretion of the police. This testing is a simple, effective and necessary method of saving lives on our roads.

Alcohol is a socially acceptable drug in Australia. As a depressant it can seriously affect drivers through drowsiness and impaired judgment, and through poor co-ordination and reaction time. In 2005 thirty-two percent of Australian road accidents were related to alcohol. The dangers of alcohol for Australian drivers are clear.

Many road deaths can be directly attributed to alcohol abuse. In New South Wales random breath testing has dramatically reduced fatalities from 653, January to June 1982, to 468 for the same period, 1983. Since its introduction preventative random breath testing reduced road accidents and fatalities more than successfully. Innocent people are in danger from drivers influenced by alcohol. Innocent drivers, passengers, riders and pedestrians, particularly the very old and the very young, are put at risk by drunken drivers. Random breath testing helps provide vital protection for these people, as s their right.

Road laws are intended to promote safety, as are laws governing random breath test. Each serves a protective function by reducing injury and death. Random breath testing should therefore be an important component of road laws for all states.

In order to combat alcohol abuse by drivers, to reduce the loss of innocent lives and to make our road laws work for us, we must have random breath testing. Our lives may depend on it.

Exercise 11.2: Constructing an argumentative essay

The question below requires a fully drafted essay.

* There is a case for the adoption of English language as an official second language in Korea. Do you agree?
(This argument should involve some rebuttal of counter-arguments during the development of your case.)

CHECKLIST

- Have I defined key terms in the question?
- Have I stated my contention at the start of the essay?
- Have I developed this contention through the body paragraph topics and supported it with relevant examples?
- Have I rebutted the main counter-arguments?
- Are my conclusions logical and supported by what has gone before?

Argumentative
Essays for Evaluation

The argumentative essay question set for each of the three essays was: 'Should capital punishment be re-introduced in Australia?'

Argumentative Essay A

'A killer. A motive. A victim. A murder.' This is the type of plot used in the romanticized Sherlock Holmes books, set m the 1890s. Murder, then, seemed such a civilized affair. It was where the killer would spend weeks planning how to commit the murder and how to get away unseen. Such intricate planning today is virtually unheard of. It is more a case of hit and run or stalk, attack, rape then kill. Such acts of barbarism are almost a daily occurrence. It is barbarism that man is gradually returning to. Of course I only accuse elements of our society that perform these inhuman aggressive acts on their fellow man but there are many such individuals throughout Australia.

It is not the act of aggression that we are concerned with, it is how we intend to deal with the aggressor. Australia does not have as high an incidence of murder as the United States, the murder capital of the world, but the figures are high enough for concern. Hardly a week goes by without us reading about some attack, whether it is in the form of rape or murder. The question is, if the government were to reinstate execution as a punishment for such crimes, would this stop the killings? In the United States, the executioner puts criminals to death, but the murders continue. Many of the most brutal attacks are performed by the mentally unstable, and to such individuals death has no meaning. To trace a killer one must think as they do. The state executioner brings death, but also more detailed investigations. If a person is falsely convicted he is, at present, sent to jai1. If by chance the real culprit is discovered, he is released. Death is not so lenient. So capital punishment is not the answer to the murder problem in Australia.

Or is it? Someone who kills for the first time finds it hard. The second time he finds it easier. The third time even easier!After that his moral standards are non-existent, and killing becomes a natural function. Such a person could be stopped from killing the first time if the consequence of his capture was death.

Considering the amount of injustice in the justice system, the death sentence would recall the need for more thorough investigations, as there could not be a shadow of a doubt in the judge's mind as he passes the ultimate sentence. This would stop the aforementioned false convictions.

So, the death sentence is the answer to the murder problem in Australia. The essayist is either for or against, and should clearly state his or her point of view, but that is only one person's opinion The only way to really find out if there is a case for capital punishment in Australia is to put the question to the populace, as it is we who are both the aggressors and the victims of aggression.

Argumentative Essay B

In Australia today, the incidence of horrific and repeated crimes against society has produced d great number of victims, both living and dead. If victims are to be put before the most serious, offenders, and people are not to lose faith in the rule of law, capital punishment must be re-introduced in this country.

Capital punishment is the punishment of a crime by death. This has not been used in Australia since 1967. Since that time, however the number of cold, savage crimes of murder has increased dramatically. This increase has been paralleled by a go-soft-on-offenders approach on the part of authorities, at great cost to victims.

The nature of the most serious crimes in Australia has changed significantly since the abolition of capital punishment, and a new category of murder now stands above all the rest. The Hoddle Street case, the Cobby murder and recent executions in Queensland demonstrate that massacres of innocent civilians do happen here, and that execution and torture are part of Australian crime now. One of the chilling implications of this is that we are no longer safe from the excesses we see in American society. The legal outcomes of our own cases are equally important in terms of the public's perceptions of justice, particularly where such serious offenders are eventually to re-enter the society from which innocent victims were cruelly taken.

In coping with the most serious murders, state governments have allowed the rehabilitation of offenders to overshadow their punishment, a trend that has been noted by an uneasy public. While murderers are groomed for re-entry to society, victims' families wait helplessly for a repeat of the original crime. At present in Australia, the most severe crimes against humanity are not met with the most severe punishments.

According to the civil rights lobby, capital punishment is legalized murder. No crime, they argue, is great enough to justify the offender's loss of life. In any case, there is the danger that the wrong person will be forced to pay that price. This line of reasoning places great value on the lives of serious offenders, but little value on the actual and potential victims. True, the courts are not perfect, and certainly public opinion is not always rational, but we must establish some absolute values and be prepared to defend them with the use of the severest penalties. Rarely, innocent people may be sent to their death under such a system, but there are far fewer of these than those innocents who die at the hands of re-offenders. Execution means the worst offenders lose their second chance, and the authority of law is enhanced in the public eye.

Here in Australia we take the rule of law for granted, but in America the lines are not so clearly drawn, especially in the wake of recent actions by vigilantes. There is clearly a danger that where courts are not permitted to apply the ultimate sanction, civilians may do it in the name of justice. If so, the status of the courts will suffer.

It would be foolish to deny that there are strong arguments for and against capital punishment, yet we should not deny that the terms of reference of the debate have changed since the 1960s, when massacres happened in other countries. Even with the risks, the worst murderers should earn the worst punishment, and we should not feel ashamed to punish such offenders. This approach will bring us as close as we are going to get to justice.

Argumentative Essay C

Capital punishment is the punishment of a crime by death. In Australia it has been abolished, the last hanging being in Victoria in 1967. Today, the death sentence is replaced by life imprisonment, which is generally twenty years minus parole. Some people do not think that life imprisonment is enough. They would prefer the defendant to be put to death. Would death be good enough?

After a serious crime, many people demand the death sentence, but this is purely an emotional reaction. These people are not thinking rationally about the issue; they are seeking revenge. The death sentence is as barbaric as the original crime; it is legalized murder. History has shown that capital punishment is not a deterrent. A person who plans a murder does not consider that he will be caught, and a crime of passion committed on the spur of the moment also does not take into account the consequences.

If someone is hanged and then later is found innocent, he has been murdered by society. A person jai1ed can be at least partly compensated for the ordeal. When a person is given the death sentence, his trauma spreads to his family and friends, and also the officials, the judge and the jury who send him to the gallows. This trauma is magnified many times if it is later proved that the accused was innocent.

Capital punishment is barbaric revenge that really achieves nothing. It is dangerous to administer the death sentence because it may be a big mistake that cannot be undone. The situation cannot be retrieved; it is a final decision. It is far better that five guilty men go free than one innocent man be executed.

In today's society, the crime rate has risen rapidly to the stage where some measure must be taken in order to deter criminals. There is definitely a case for capital punishment to be re-introduced to Australian society as it has the potential to dramatically reduce the crime rate. Perhaps the threat of such a severe punishment would give killers second thoughts about murdering, and civilians would live safely, knowing that murderers could not escape from jail to continue their killing. As well as this, hardworking, honest taxpayers would not be forced to pay for the upkeep of killers.

Introducing the death penalty would deter criminals and cut the crime rate. People would have second thoughts about committing murder, rape or child molestation if such a severe punishment was in existence. The thought of possible execution would in many cases destroy all criminal desire.

Re-introducing capital punishment would also mean that victims of such crimes as rape could live in safety and protection, knowing that their attackers could not possibly re-enter society. Knowing this would be a great comfort to many, and indeed the death penalty would give many people a chance to regain a normal lifestyle.

Hardworking, honest taxpayers are the people who pay for the upkeep of prisoners. It is they who feed and clothe the criminals. Society has absolutely no need for hardened criminals, so the government is simply wasting taxpayers' money in paying for the costs of keeping murderers alive.

Somewhere, however, we must draw the line between those who deserve merely a jail term and those who deserve a death sentence. It is criminals, such as rapists, child molesters, drug traffickers and cold-blooded killers that should be executed, whereas a jaii sentence is sufficient for other offenders.

It should be kept in mind, however, that capital punishment is completely irreversible. Thus, if an executed prisoner is later found to be innocent, nothing can be done to remedy such a tragic situation. The knowledge of their innocence is hardly likely to ease the suffering of the family and friends of the victim. In effect, an innocent person has been legally murdered, therefore, must the executioner then be murdered for killing an innocent person?

In England, in the 1950s, Timothy Evans was hanged after being found guilty of a series of murders. After his death, it was proved that Evans was actually innocent, and a man by the name of Christie was the killer. Also, in the case of Lindy Chamberlain, a woman was found guilty and sentenced to life imprisonment for the murder of her baby daughter. Later, however, she was found to be innocent, and was released from prison with a pardon. If capital punishment had been in operation in this case, the dreadful mistake could not have been corrected, and much added suffering would have resulted.

Due to the fact that capital punishment would mean a reduction in taxes, an increase in the safety and security of many people, and an effective deterrent to many criminals, capital punishment is a favorable idea. There is definitely a case for it in Australia. If brought into existence, however, the law would have to be extremely clear that only those proved guilty beyond all possible doubt should be executed. This rule must be strictly adhered to, or innocent lives could be taken.

Chapter 12

Common Faults in Written Expression

Avoiding Errors

The intention of this chapter is not to provide a systematic examination of grammar or structure, but to point out those errors most commonly made by students. The exercises are designed to help you identify and correct errors, and ultimately achieve a greater clarity and simplicity of expression.

Colloquialisms and Slang

Essays should be written in formal English. Therefore, there should be no short-cuts, such as contractions, nor any casual or slang expressions. For example, you can say 'firstly' but not 'for starters'. 'Could not' is acceptable, but not 'couldn't'. Another example: you can say 'without doubt' but not 'no mistake'.

Colloquial and slang expressions may appear in essays only as part of quotations that are relevant to the purpose of the essay.

Exercise 12.1: Avoiding colloquialisms and slang

Find formal expressions for the following:

(1) Pretty good
(2) a fair bit
(3) caused a few hassles
(4) mucked up the plan
(5) just the thing
(6) finished up
(7) for a while there
(8) fair enough
(9) didn't kid herself
(10) wasn't really the best

Generally speaking, it is best to avoid informal expressions altogether, even in those instances where you 'admit' to informality by placing colloquialisms or slang in inverted commas. If you are unsure about the best way to convey your meaning to the reader, turn to a dictionary or thesaurus. You should not settle for a vague expression when a precise and appropriate one is close at hand.

Cliche

A *cliche* is a worn-out, over-used term that has lost its originality and impact. For instance, 'fall on deaf ears', 'a foregone conclusion' and 'in this day and age' are all cliches.

Exercise 12.2: Avoiding cliches

Find more original expressions for the following cliches:

(1) a whole new ball game
(2) in this day and age
(3) tarred with the same brush
(4) Don't worry, be happy!
(5) to skate on thin ice
(6) as cool as a cucumber
(7) as dry as dust
(8) Today is the first day of the rest of your life.
(9) in the same boat
(10) What goes around comes around.
(11) *Carpe diem*
(12) Always look on the bright side of life

Tautology

Tautology occurs when the same thing is said twice. Examples of this include 'look back in retrospect' and 'a three-part trilogy.'

Exercise 12.3: Avoiding tautology

Remove the tautology from each of the following sentences:

(1) The motorist was told to return back to the highway

(2) Several dogs fought over one single bone

(3) The bowler did not receive a favorable approval from the umpire.

(4) Voters in the election were faced with two alternative options.

(5) In my opinion, I think that the show should be repeated again after such a successful opening night

Ambiguity

Ambiguity leaves readers with a choice of two or more meanings when only one is intended. For instance, if a doctor tells a patient that he 'will never be the same again' after an operation, the patient has no single meaning to rely on. Ambiguity is perhaps the most difficult problem to avoid for many students because simple errors, such as a misplaced comma, can mean the difference between a clear meaning and an ambiguous one.

Exercise 12.4: Avoiding ambiguity

Remove the ambiguity from each of the following sentences:

(1) The woman patted the dog as she ran past.
(2) An alligator was behind the animals waiting to feed.
(3) The politician held the koala and he urinated in front of the cameras.
(4) A band was at the station and the train went through it.
(5) Have you eaten mother?

Punctuation Errors

Essays often have long sentences that may contain several ideas or that involve complex explanations. If clarity of meaning is to be preserved, commas, apostrophes and quotation marks need to be used accurately and consistently. Commas are used to mark a natural pause in a sentence, to mark an aside from your main flow of ideas and to separate items in a list. Apostrophes are used to show ownership and to show contraction. Quotation marks are used when quoting the actual words that someone said, thought or wrote. Any punctuation associated with the words being quoted must appear inside the quotation marks.

Exercise 12.5: Using commas

Insert commas where necessary:

(1) On leaving camp George hastily donned an officer's coat.
(2) Outside the soldiers were resting.
(3) Gonzalez the athlete who had crawled across the continent was not impressed by the media coverage he received.
(4) 'Come hither Sir Horace' her eyes seemed to say.
(5) Haig although originally against the idea gave his consent.
(6) The fire destroyed all crops in the area most of the live-stock all of the timber structures and many farm vehicles.
(7) Having seen the destruction caused the lives lost and the cost incurred the generals decided to withdraw.

(8) 'I want to rule Europe' he told his staff 'but first we must win it'.

Exercise 12.6: Using apostrophes

Insert an apostrophe where necessary:

(1) Jane wants to clear the yard of Rovers collection of bones.
(2) Bills bike arrives today but he wont need it yet.
(3) Its wonderful to see the armadillo in its natural home.
(4) The childrens presents are under the tree.
(5) Womens sizes werent available in our citys largest store.

Exercise 12.7: Using quotation marks

Insert quotation marks where necessary in the following sentences.

(1) Stop that man! called the inspector.
(2) Men are made bad by bad treatment, Kelly is reported to have said.
(3) You're wrong, the minister told newsmen, if you think this is merely a publicity stunt.
(4) Men and women of Australia, he addressed the crowd, it is a crisis that we face, the people stared and listened, and only you can avert it by voting for us.

(5) This is it! I thought to myself, and jumped out of the plane. Yahoo! we all screamed as our hands linked to form a star.

(6) Early in the novel, Ged had been warned of the powers of the darkness when Ogion told him the girl herself is half witch already.

Weaknesses in Sentence Structure

Agreement of verbs, the non-sentence and the run-on sentence are the most common structural problems for most students.

Exercise 12.8: Using the right tense

Verbs must agree with their subjects in tense and number. Correct the verbs used wrongly in the following sentences:

(1) 'No one,' he warned us, 'have the right to interfere m this matter.'
(2) The company have made good profits this year.
(3) Neither of the alternatives facing the council are worth considering.
(4) There was only seven officers left alive after the revolt.
(5) 'Files on Corruption'have sold well in bookstores this week.
(6) On our last camping trip we were faced with a terrible storm, our supplies were low and our boat is missing.
(7) Although he reached Moscow, Napoleon has no surrender to gloat over, no army to face, and on his return to the west, he will be caught by the bitter Russian winter.

Exercise 12.9: Avoiding muddled sentences

Rewrite each of the following non-sentences so that each becomes a sentence expressing a complete, unambiguous thought. Feel free to make changes, but remember to preserve the intended meaning of the original.

(1) On examining the goods they were found to be defective.

(2) Reading through the poem on a more detailed level where the images become clearer.

(3) Billy, the central character in this novel about life in a northern industrial town.

(4) Since the play is set in the present, with characters and events which are familiar to us.

(5) Rivalry between the two leaders, mutual suspicion of each other and a lack of will to cause major changes on both sides.

Exercise 12.10: Avoiding long sentences

Using at least two sentences in each case, rewrite each of these long sentences:

(1) Robin Hood took money from the rich and then, after keeping a nominal agent's commission, gave it to the poor and the people who received it were the poor woodcutters and the pretty widows.

(2) This novel is about the problems of prejudice and injustice that the negroes of the South had to endure and the man who suffered most was Tom because he was an innocent man who lost his life at the hands of white guards.

(3) Igor was Dracula's valet, his job was to do all the unromantic chores around the castle, his physique was very distinctive with the obligatory hump, large eyes and a disconcerting twitch at the side of the mouth.

(4) Pirates, in the main, were unlicensed raiders who could expect no help from their governments if they were caught and sometimes women pirates joined the lucrative business in the Caribbean.

(5) Mao, Tse-Tung took the communists on a long walk to escape the enemy which was Chiang Kai-Shek and his men surrounded the communist base and the escape allowed Mao to establish a new base in the north.

Protecting Your Meaning

Try to be simple, clear and straightforward in your essay expression. By doing this, you will be able to hold your reader's attention and interest. Here are some hints for the protection of meaning:

Hints

1. Follow the points in your plan.
2. Deal with one thing at a time.
3. Avoid side-tracks.
4. Try not to squeeze too much into one sentence.
5. Be aware of the verbs that control each sentence.
6. Remember that words such as 'because', 'since', 'although' and 'while' must join two parts of a sentence.
7. Give each paragraph a topic sentence.
8. Check that punctuation preserves your intended meaning.
9. Avoid big, flashy words that serve no useful purpose in transmitting your meaning.
10. Re-read your essay later, as errors will stand out more clearly then.

Chapter 13

Words of Transition

For Writing Good Essays

WORDS OF TRANSITION

Purpose	Transitional Words
To add	also, and, and then, too, plus, in addition, furthermore, moreover, again, on top of that, another, first, second, third
To put in time order	now, then, before, after, afterward, earlier, later, immediately, soon, next, in a few days, meanwhile, gradually, suddenly, finally, previously
To put in space order	near, near to, far from, in front of, beside, in the rear of, beyond, above, below, to the right, to the left, around, surrounding, on one side, inside, outside, alongside

Purpose	Transitional Words
To compare	in the same way, similarly, just like, just as, likewise
To contrast	but, still, however, on the other hand, on the contrary, yet, nevertheless, despite, in spite of, even though, in contrast, instead
To show cause and effect	because, since, so, consequently, as a result, therefore, then, accordingly, hence, thus
To show purpose	for this reason, for this purpose, so that this may happen
To emphasize	indeed, in fact, surely, necessarily, certainly, without any doubt, in any event, truly, again, to repeat
To give examples	for example, for instance, as an illustration, specifically, to be specific, as proof
To summarize	in summary, in conclusion, as I have shown, as has been stated, in other words, in brief, to sum up, thus, so

Chapter 14

Essay Collection

More Sample Essays for Writing Good Essays

Basic Essay

Outline three ways in which sport brings us benefits. (300 words)

STRUCTURE introduction, which includes: · a lead-in idea (not essential) · a statement of essay question · indication to the reader of what you are going to talk about (an 'essay map')	Not everybody likes sport but most people agree that participation in sporting activity benefits us in many ways. The most obvious advantages are physical, but there are also social and personal benefits.	**LANGUAGE FEATURES** the writer keeps a distance from the topic-not personal feelings and experiences formal not informal everyday language
	In the first place, all sport involves regular physical activity and, because of this, it helps us become healthier and fitter. Regular activity, for example, develops muscle tone and therefore improves body strength. It also fosters good breathing techniques and so improves our lung capacity. Furthermore, it reduces the risk of heart disease and high blood pressure. Also, because exercise burns up fat, sport is an ideal way to maintain a good body weight. This, in turn, is important for the prevention of other health problems.	linking words, e.g. 'also', 'secondly'
one paragraph per main idea	Secondly, sport brings us many social benefits. Many people, for example, form strong and lasting friendships through participation in sport. It also teaches important lessons for getting on with others. These include sportsmanship, leadership, and the importance of teamwork.	many nouns such as 'sportsmanship', 'importance' etc. which help us pack a lot of meaning into a sentence
topic sentences which tell the reader what the paragraph is about	Thirdly, sport helps us develop personally-that is, mentally and emotionally. One of its most valuable aspects is that it teaches us to deal with both winning and losing. Some people believe competition is a bad thing, but if it teaches this important lesson it can be extremely useful. Another personal benefit is that it provides an opportunity to set and achieve goals. For some people this might mean winning medals and breaking records, but for most, it means striving for their 'personal best'.	talking about people in general, not individuals often the use of 'we' or 'us' to talk about people in general
conclusion: · sums up content · gives no new information · gives writer's view of the topic in some way	These are just some of the advantages of participating in sport. Most sportsmen and sportswomen probably do not consciously think of these benefits when they play sport. Like me, they play sport for one simple reason-it is good fun.	complete sentences

Topic: Outline three ways in which sport brings us benefits.

Not everybody likes sport but most people agree that participation in sporting activity benefits us in many ways. The most obvious advantages are physical, but there are also social and personal benefits.

In the first place, all sport involves regular physical activity and, because of this, it helps us become healthier and fitter. Regular activity, for example, develops muscle tone and therefore improves body strength. It also fosters good breathing techniques and so improves our lung capacity. Furthermore, it reduces the risk of heart disease and high blood pressure. Also, because exercise burns up fat, sport is an ideal way to maintain a good body weight. This, in turn, is important for the prevention of other health problems.

Secondly, sport brings us many social benefits. Many people, for example, form strong and lasting friendships through participation in sport. It also teaches important lessons for getting on with others. These include sportsmanship, leadership, and the importance of teamwork.

Thirdly, sport helps us develop personally-that is, mentally and emotionally. One of its most valuable aspects is that it teaches us to deal with both winning and losing. Some people believe competition is a bad thing, but if it teaches this important lesson it can be extremely useful. Another personal benefit is that it provides an opportunity to set and achieve goals. For some people this might mean winning medals and breaking records, but for most, it means striving for their 'personal best'.

These are just some of the advantages of participating in sport. Most sportsmen and sportswomen probably do not consciously think of these benefits when they play sport. Like me, they play sport for one simple reason - it is good fun.

Discussion Essay

'Girls and boys should be educated separately in secondary school.' Discuss. (350 words)

STRUCTURE		**LANGUAGE FEATURES**
introduction, which includes: · lead-in idea (optional) · essay question · 'essay map' (generally no view at this stage. View comes at end)	When children reach the end of primary school, one important question their parents have to consider is whether it would be better to send them to a single-sex school or a mixed-sex (coeducational) school. They have to weigh up many points on both sides of the argument-both educational and social.	distance from the topic-not personal formal language no emotional language
balanced discussion of issue	One of the main arguments for segregated education is the fact that boys demand more of their teachers' time. Firstly, boys need more discipline because they are more likely to misbehave in class. Secondly, they get more attention than girls do, because they tend to speak up more in class. If girls are educated separately, they might have more of their teachers' time, and so learn faster and better.	linking words, e.g. 'firstly', 'secondly'
paragraphs, which give arguments for or against (Some discussion essays are not clearly 'for' and 'against'-they are a general discussion of ideas)	Another argument for separate schooling is that it gives students a better chance to do well in subjects where one sex or the other traditionally does better. Girls sometimes think it is not feminine to do well in maths and science. Boys sometimes think it is not masculine or 'macho' to do well in expressive subjects such as English. If they are in segregated classes, they may not be so affected by these ideas, and so be more likely to perform at their best.	talking about people in general, not individual, e.g. 'girls', 'boys', 'teachers'
	These arguments may appear strong reasons to send a girl or boy to a single-sex school, but there are also reasons to favour mixed-sex schooling. The strongest argument is that it prepares students better for the real world, especially the world of work where in general people have to work with both sexes. Both males and females need to learn to get on with one another, and school is probably the best place to learn these important social skills.	words such as 'may', 'can' and 'probably' reflect that the issue is debatable-not black and white
top sentences	Another argument in favour of coeducation is that both boys and girls can have a good effect on the classroom. Boys may behave more appropriately if there are girls in the classroom, and girls may learn to be more outspoken if they see boys behaving in this way.	pronouns to link ideas, e.g. 'they', 'these'
conclusion: · sums up content · gives no new information · states view on essay question (for, against or some position in between)	Overall the social arguments for combined schooling outweigh the mostly educational arguments for segregated schooling. Education is not only about learning facts and figures but also about learning how to survive socially. Coeducation is certainly the best system for teaching this important lesson.	complete sentences

Topic: 'Girls and boys should be educated separately in secondary school.' Discuss.

When children reach the end of primary school, one important question their parents have to consider is whether it would be better to send them to a single-sex school or a mixed-sex (coeducational) school. They have to weigh up many points on both sides of the argument-both educational and social.

One of the main arguments for segregated education is the fact that boys demand more of their teachers' time. Firstly, boys need more discipline because they are more likely to misbehave in class. Secondly, they get more attention than girls do, because they tend to speak up more in class. If girls are educated separately, they might have more of their teachers' time, and so learn faster and better.

Another argument for separate schooling is that it gives students a better chance to do well in subjects where one sex or the other traditionally does better. Girls sometimes think it is not feminine to do well in maths and science. Boys sometimes think it is not masculine or 'macho' to do well in expressive subjects such as English. If they are in segregated classes, they may not be so affected by these ideas, and so be more likely to perform at their best.

These arguments may appear strong reasons to send a girl or boy to a single-sex school, but there are also reasons to favour mixed-sex schooling. The strongest argument is that it prepares students better for the real world, especially the world of work where in general people have to work with both sexes. Both males and females need to learn to get on with one another, and school is probably the best place to learn these important social skills.

Another argument in favour of coeducation is that both boys and girls can have a good effect on the classroom. Boys may behave more appropriately if there are girls in the classroom, and girls may learn to be more outspoken if they see boys behaving in this way.

Overall the social arguments for combined schooling outweigh the mostly educational arguments for segregated schooling. Education is not only about learning facts and figures but also about learning how to survive socially. Coeducation is certainly the best system for teaching this important lesson.

Descriptive Essay

Write a description of a crowd scene you have experienced, e.g. concert, a sports game or a street crowd.

STRUCTURE	The game	LANGUAGE FEATURES
. orientation to scene by reference to action, location, time etc.	'GIIIRD-LAA, GIIIRD-LAA, GIIIRD-LAA, GIIIRD-LAA, ' 'Whumpf.' And it flies off into the sparkling sun, spinning towards the goalposts. But it's gone too far and they're up. Pimply teenagers, wether-beaten old men, women, kids-all screeching fanatics-all on their feet cheering and clapping. They've done their job. Played their part in the weekly ritual. With their jeering they've successfully put a young player off his game and saved their team two valuable points.	opening word, which instantly capture reader's interest pronouns to refer to people and things
different aspects of the scene, e.g. the people, the stadium, the players	The whistle blows and the hard fought conflict is on again. Individual differences are forgotten under the colours of the teams. Old are young, meek are strong, all are united. One team battles it out against the other in the grandstand. It's a match of wit and passion, of insults and physical threats, but curiously it rarely comes to blows.	descriptive language to create images in reader's mind-visual, sound etc.
	On the grassy hill the smell of beer and chips overwhelms. No one can tell who is going for who. All that matters is that you are yelling your lungs out: 'Are yer blind or sumthin?' 'Where'd yer learn ta ref?', 'Offside? OFFSIDE? Ya gotta be kidding', 'Get your rule book out ref'.	
only some details included selection of detail to suit writing purpose, e.g. to give a sense of mood, to amuse etc.	An old lady leaps from her wheelchair, waving her blanket in the air as her favourite player goes crashing over the line. She can barely see the scoreboard through her inch-thick glasses, but she knows she's in front and there's not long till the full-time hooter.	writer here writes as if he is an outsider looking in and uses third person ('he', 'they'), not first person ('I', 'we')
	A group of boys come sprinting past her on their way to the goalposts, desperate to touch the ball as it zooms through the uprights: Leaping over fans, scattering bags, chip cartons and other debris as they go. They burn with the idea. On, to touch that ball.	not always complete sentences-words and phrases used to create impact
	A father whisks a bundle away as they thunder past and hold it high. It's almost unrecognizable as a baby girl under the layers of jersey, beanie, scarf and other team gear. She looks more like a flag. Her father seems to think so too and waves her in the air as number 12 swings his foot. The ball sails high again and the flags are up.	consistent use of whatever tense is chosen-here present tense is used to make scene seem closer
conclusion, which brings the description to an end, e.g. by returning to the beginning in some way sometimes a comment or evaluation of the scene and elements	This time the hecklers don't get to him and he grabs back the two points he lost to them earlier. The stadium is ringing with his name as his two precious points are posted on the scoreboard. This time it is his own supporters singing his name. 'Girdler, Girdler, Girdler.' **William McLean**	many action verbs, e.g. 'swings', 'grabs'

Topic: Write a description of a crowd scene you have experienced, e.g. concert, a sports game or a street crowd.

The game

'GIIIRD-LAA, GIIIRD-LAA, GIIIRD-LAA, GIIIRD-LAA, ' 'Whumpf.' And it flies off into the sparkling sun, spinning towards the goalposts. But it's gone too far and they're up. Pimply teenagers, wether-beaten old men, women, kids-all screeching fanatics-all on their feet cheering and clapping. They've done their job. Played their part in the weekly ritual. With their jeering they've successfully put a young player off his game and saved their team two valuable points.

The whistle blows and the hard fought conflict is on again. Individual differences are forgotten under the colours of the teams. Old are young, meek are strong, all are united. One team battles it out against the other in the grandstand. It's a match of wit and passion, of insults and physical threats, but curiously it rarely comes to blows.

On the grassy hill the smell of beer and chips overwhelms. No one can tell who is going for who. All that matters is that you are yelling your lungs out: 'Are yer blind or sumthin?' 'Where'd yer learn ta ref?', 'Offside? OFFSIDE? Ya gotta be kidding', 'Get your rule book out ref'.

An old lady leaps from her wheelchair, waving her blanket in the air as her favourite player goes crashing over the line. She can barely see the scoreboard through her inch-thick glasses, but she knows she's in front and there's not long till the full-time hooter.

A group of boys come sprinting past her on their way to the goalposts, desperate to touch the ball as it zooms through the uprights: Leaping over fans, scattering bags, chip cartons and other debris as they go. They burn with the idea. On, to touch that ball.

A father whisks a bundle away as they thunder past and hold it high. It's almost unrecognizable as a baby girl under the layers of jersey, beanie, scarf and other team gear. She looks more like a flag. Her father seems to think so too and waves her in the air as number 12 swings his foot. The ball sails high again and the flags are up.

This time the hecklers don't get to him and he grabs back the two points he lost to them earlier. The stadium is ringing with his name as his two precious points are posted on the scoreboard. This time it is his own supporters singing his name. 'Girdler, Girdler, Girdler.'

William McLean

Biography

STRUCTURE	Martin Luther King	LANGUAGE FEATURES
introduction, which gives name of person and why he/she was famous	Martin Luther King was the leader of the Civil Rights Movement against racism in the United States of America during the 1950s and 1960s. Tragically, at the age of 39 he was shot dead.	formal language
focus on recounting facts about person's life	King was born in 1929 in Atlanta, Georgia, in the deep south of the USA, where the segregation of black people and white people was a way of life. In most southern states at that time, laws made it a crime for black people to use the same restaurants, schools and even sections of public transport, as white people.	mostly objective language but may be some subjective language which show writer's attitude to person
paragraphs about different stages or aspects of person's life-generally in chronological sequence	King became a Baptist minister, and in his church spoke out against segregation and racism. But in 1955, something happened which led to a far greater role for him in fighting racial injustice. A woman called Rosa Parks in Montgomery, Alabama, refused to move for a white woman on a bus and was arrested. From that moment onwards, King became a leader of his people across the nation.	time phrases to show chronological sequence of events, e.g. 'in 1955' focus on specific people and events
careful selection of detail about person's life	His first step was leading a bus boycott in Montgomery which successfully led to a change in the law about segregated seating. He went on to lead other blacks in a campaign for freedom. This included sit-ins at segregated lunch counter, demonstrations, rallies and freedom rides (bus rides to places where there were particular racial problems). The largest rally was on 28 August 1963, when 200 000 people marched together through Washington, DC.	
	King became well-known for his powers of oratory. When he spoke, people listened. His words at the Washington rally still have the power to stir our hearts and minds: 'I have a dream that one day this nation will rise up and live out the true meaning of its creed: We hold these truths to be self-evident that all men are created equal...'.	pronouns to link ideas through text, e.g. 'he', 'his' past tense, e.g. 'was born', 'became'
	King's success was in part to do with his non-violent approach. Because of this, he had support from both blacks and whites. In1963 he was named Time Magazine's Man of the Year and in1963 he received the Nobel Peace Prize.	
specific information about time and place	In 1968 King was in Memphis, Tennessee, supporting striking sanitation workers. There' on 4 April, he was shot dead by James Earl Ray, a white ex-convict.	
may or may not be conclusion, but last paragraph often includes some comment on person's life or contribution	King's assassination rocked the nation and the world. Black and white people alike mourned the loss of this brilliant, courageous man who devoted his life to his people and his country, and who had the power to move an audience like no other.	

Martin Luther King

Martin Luther King was the leader of the Civil Rights Movement against racism in the United States of America during the 1950s and 1960s. Tragically, at the age of 39 he was shot dead.

King was born in 1929 in Atlanta, Georgia, in the deep south of the USA, where the segregation of black people and white people was a way of life. In most southern states at that time, laws made it a crime for black people to use the same restaurants, schools and even sections of public transport, as white people.

King became a Baptist minister, and in his church spoke out against segregation and racism. But in 1955, something happened which led to a far greater role for him in fighting racial injustice. A woman called Rosa Parks in Montgomery, Alabama, refused to move for a white woman on a bus and was arrested. From that moment onwards, King became a leader of his people across the nation.

His first step was leading a bus boycott in Montgomery which successfully led to a change in the law about segregated seating. He went on to lead other blacks in a campaign for freedom. This included sit-ins at segregated lunch counter, demonstrations, rallies and freedom rides (bus rides to places where there were particular racial problems). The largest rally was on 28 August 1963, when 200 000 people marched together through Washington, DC.

King's success was in part to do with his non-violent approach. Because of this, he had support from both blacks and whites. In1963 he was named Time Magazine's Man of the Year and in1963 he received the Nobel Peace Prize.

In 1968 King was in Memphis, Tennessee, supporting striking sanitation workers. There' on 4 April, he was shot dead by James Earl Ray, a white ex-convict.

King's assassination rocked the nation and the world. Black and white people alike mourned the loss of this brilliant, courageous man who devoted his life to his people and his country, and who had the power to move an audience like no other.

Speech

Choose a controversial topic and prepare a two-minute speech arguing your point of view.

STRUCTURE opening, which quickly catches the audience's attention, and at the same time establishes the topic and purpose of speech	If we kill the killer, we too deserve to be killed. Good morning class. Capital punishment. Once again, after another horrific crime, this topic is back under discussion. So, should we reintroduce it or not? I think not.	**LANGUAGE FEATURES** address the audience, e.g. 'ladies and gentlemen', 'class'
ideas organised as appropriate to purpose of speech-here arguments to support point of view	To execute someone for a crime is to follow the ancient custom of 'an eye for an eye and a tooth for a tooth'. In other words, it is pure revenge. Think for a moment what sort of example this sets for the community at large. What does it say to them about dealing with conflict and hardship? A good message would you say?	more repetition and restatement of ideas than in writing-to help your listeners follow the ideas
ideas not always fully developed as in an essay-because of time limits and need to limit amount of detail for audience	Even if there is no doubt that someone has murdered, should the state stoop to that level and murder as well? If a convicted murderer is sentenced to life imprisonment, that person is no longer a danger to society. There is absolutely no need to execute criminals to punish them. Imprisonment is punishment enough. And imprisonment offers the hope of rehabilitation-surely something we should be aiming for.	personal language, e.g. 'I', 'you', 'we', 'us'
	Capital punishment is certainly not a deterrent. People who commit serious crimes don't think about the consequences before doing so. In the US, where capital punishment exists in some states, the murder rate is still climbing. Britain has abolished the death penalty, as has Australia, and our murder statistics per head of population are lower than in those US state. Considerably lower.	not always full sentences-phrases and isolated words used for effect
	The death penalty is a cop out for dealing with our social problems. A quick fix. The roots of crime lie in poverty, abuse, racism, injustice. Society needs to look at these causes and deal with them. People who commit vicious crimes have often suffered from neglect, cruelty, emotional trauma, violence, abandonment, lack of love and a host of destructive social conditions. Is it fair to hold these people fully accountable for their wrongdoing? Is not society at least partly to blame?	often some colloquial, everyday language, e.g. 'cop out' use of questions to set up a conversation with listeners
	It is not capital punishment that will make society safe from violent crime but attention to its needs. Killing will not stop crime. Caring will. Let us show mercy even to those who have shown none, to return good for evil. For to err is human, to forgive is divine.	
conclusion: · relates to the content and purpose of speech · may include a question, a warning, a quotation	Capital punishment is inhuman, barbaric and, in my eyes at least, legalized murder.	

Topic: Choose a controversial topic and prepare a two-minute speech arguing your point of view.

If we kill the killer, we too deserve to be killed. Good morning class. Capital punishment. Once again, after another horrific crime, this topic is back under discussion. So, should we reintroduce it or not? I think not.

To execute someone for a crime is to follow the ancient custom of 'an eye for an eye and a tooth for a tooth'. In other words, it is pure revenge. Think for a moment what sort of example this sets for the community at large. What does it say to them about dealing with conflict and hardship?

A good message would you say?

Even if there is no doubt that someone has murdered, should the state stoop to that level and murder as well? If a convicted murderer is sentenced to life imprisonment, that person is no longer a danger to society. There is absolutely no need to execute criminals to punish them. Imprisonment is punishment enough. And imprisonment offers the hope of rehabilitation-surely something we should be aiming for.

Capital punishment is certainly not a deterrent. People who commit serious crimes don't think about the consequences before doing so. In the US, where capital punishment exists in some states, the murder rate is still climbing. Britain has abolished the death penalty, as has Australia, and our murder statistics per head of population are lower than in those US state. Considerably lower.

The death penalty is a cop out for dealing with our social problems. A quick fix. The roots of crime lie in poverty, abuse, racism, injustice. Society needs to look at these causes and deal with them. People who commit vicious crimes have often suffered from neglect, cruelty, emotional trauma, violence, abandonment, lack of love and a host of destructive social

conditions. Is it fair to hold these people fully accountable for their wrongdoing? Is not society at least partly to blame?
It is not capital punishment that will make society safe from violent crime but attention to its needs. Killing will not stop crime. Caring will. Let us show mercy even to those who have shown none, to return good for evil. For to err is human, to forgive is divine.

Capital punishment is inhuman, barbaric and, in my eyes at least, legalized murder.

Explanation

STRUCTURE	**The human eye**	**LANGUAGE FEATURES**
Introduction, which identifies and says something about the process being explained	The human eye is perhaps our most important sense organ. We depend upon sight more than upon any other sense to supply us with crucial information about the world we live in.	formal and impersonal language
focus on factual information relevant information only information about how or why phenomenon works-usually in the order things occur in real world	In many ways the eye operates like a camera. Light rays enter through a small area of transparent material (called the cornea). The amount of light allowed in is controlled by the widening or narrowing of the pupil which acts like a camera aperture. (The pupil is the black hole in the middle of the iris or coloured part of the eye.) The light rays are then brought into focus by the lens behind the pupil, and projected onto a membrane at the back of the eyeball. This membrane acts like the film inside the camera and is called the retina. As in a camera, the image projected is inverted (Upside-down).	most generic non-human nouns, e.g. 'the eye', 'the brain', 'impulses' technical terms, often with everyday terms to help explain them
	However, the similarity between a camera and the eye ends there. When we take a photo, we are just recording images onto film. Our eyes do much more than this. They allow us to make sense of what we see. This is because the eyes are connected to the brain. The images that are formed on the darkened black wall of the retina are converted into electrical impulses. These impulses are sent to the brain along the optic nerve, and are then converted into messages that are meaningful to us.	pronouns to link ideas through text, e.g. 'it', 'they' repetition of key words throughout text to link ideas, e.g. 'light rays' time and cause-effect relationships often passive voice, e.g. 'are sent'
	There are two particularly important things the brain does. Firstly, it puts together the separate information it receives from each eye so that we do not see double. Secondly, it learns to read the upside-down images on our retina and turn them the right way up. The brain learns to do both these things automatically when we are very young, but small babies actually do see double and upside down for a short while.	
may or may not be conclusion (depends on topic and length of explanation)	The brain also sorts out the information it gets from the two different types of light-sensitive nerve cells on the retina-rods and cones. The rods are highly sensitive to light intensity but do not register colour. The cones see colour and fine details, but only work in bright light. This is why when daylight begins to fade, our sight is less clear and colours disappear or become a green-grey or blue.	usually present tense, e.g. 'see', 'work'

Topic: The human eye

The human eye is perhaps our most important sense organ. We depend upon sight more than upon any other sense to supply us with crucial information about the world we live in.

In many ways the eye operates like a camera. Light rays enter through a small area of transparent material (called the cornea). The amount of light allowed in is controlled by the widening or narrowing of the pupil which acts like a camera aperture. (The pupil is the black hole in the middle of the iris or coloured part of the eye.) The light rays are then brought into focus by the lens behind the pupil, and projected onto a membrane at the back of the eyeball. This membrane acts like the film inside the camera and is called the retina. As in a camera, the image projected is inverted (Upside-down).

However, the similarity between a camera and the eye ends there. When we take a photo, we are just recording images onto film. Our eyes do much more than this. They allow us to make sense of what we see. This is because the eyes are connected to the brain. The images that are formed on the darkened black wall of the retina are converted into electrical impulses. These impulses are sent to the brain along the optic nerve, and are then converted into messages that are meaningful to us.

There are two particularly important things the brain does. Firstly, it puts together the separate information it receives from each eye so that we do not see double. Secondly, it learns to read the upside-down images on our retina and turn them the right way up. The brain learns to do both these things automatically when we are very young, but small babies actually do see double and upside down for a short while.

The brain also sorts out the information it gets from the two different types of light-sensitive nerve cells on the retina-rods and cones. The rods are highly sensitive to light intensity but do not register colour. The cones see colour and fine details, but only work in bright light. This is why when daylight begins to fade, our sight is less clear and colours disappear or become a green-grey or blue.

Explanation Essay

STRUCTURE		LANGUAGE FEATURES
Introduction, Which includes: l a lead-in sentence (optional) l a restatement of the essay question l a sentence that tells the reader what you are going to talk about— an essay map	It is difficult for most people to imagine life without computers. Even if we do not have a computer in our homes, computers are now a major part of our lives. Among the many areas where they have brought great benefits are medicine, communication and leisure.	The writer keeps a distance from the topic and uses no emotional language Abstract words, e.g. 'abstract', 'areas'
	Computer technology has dramatically increased the opportunities that sick and disabled people have to lead normal lives. For example, blind people can now use a laser beam to help them work out how far they are from objects. Computers have also helped people who live in the outback to get medical help quickly in an emergency. Specialists in big city hospitals can use computers linked to modems to look at X-rays and brain scans of patients a long way away. They can then give instructions to hospital staff about what to do. Sometimes this can save lives.	
Many nouns packed into a sentence		
Most Straightforward Type of essay— Focus on known, accepted facts or events one paragraph per main idea	In communication, one of the things that has changed our lives immensely has been the Internet. Businesses these days cannot survive without being connected to the Internet. If someone in an office on the other side of the world needs to send a document to someone in Australia, it would take days without a computer, but thanks to the Internet it can be done in a matter of seconds by email. Email has changed our personal lives too. Even grandparents around the world are 'logging-on' to talk to their young grandchildren far away.	Talking about people in general, not individuals Not usually any reference to 'I' or 'me' in the body
Topic sentences, Which tell the reader what the paragraph is about Examples to expand main idea of paragraph	Leisure is another aspect of everyday life that computers have improved. Many children get great enjoyment out of the many interesting and challenging computer games they can play. Although there are many games that involve violence, if the games are chosen carefully they can really help children develop thinking skills and quick reflexes. Also, when we sit down to watch a sports game on television, it is computers that bring us the many different camera angles, instant action replays and tallies of penalties.	Linking words, e.g. 'also' Complete Sentences
Conclusion: l summarizes content l gives no new information l expresses opinion on the topic	Medicine, communication and leisure are just three areas of our lives that have improved because of computers. The advantages they have brought, in my opinion, far outweigh any disadvantages.	

Topic: Many people argue that computers are taking over our lives, but most people also acknowledge the benefits that computers have brought us. Out line three ways in which computers benefit our lives. (350 words)

It is difficult for most people to imagine life without computers. Even if we do not have a computer in our homes, computers are now a major part of our lives. Among the many areas where they have brought great benefits are medicine, communication and leisure.

Computer technology has dramatically increased the opportunities that sick and disabled people have to lead normal lives. For example, blind people can now use a laser beam to help them work out how far they are from objects. Computers have also helped people who live in the outback to get medical help quickly in an emergency. Specialists in big city hospitals can use computers linked to modems to look at X-rays and brain scans of patients a long way away. They can then give instructions to hospital staff about what to do. Sometimes this can save lives.

In communication, one of the things that has changed our lives immensely has been the Internet. Businesses these days cannot survive without being connected to the Internet. If someone in an office on the other side of the world needs to send a document to someone in Australia, it would take days without a computer, but thanks to the Internet it can be done in a matter of seconds by email. Email has changed our personal lives too. Even grandparents around the world are 'logging-on' to talk to their young grandchildren far away.

Leisure is another aspect of everyday life that computers have improved. Many children get great enjoyment out of the many interesting and challenging computer games they can play. Although there are many games that involve violence, if the games are chosen carefully they can really help children develop thinking skills and quick reflexes. Also, when we sit down to watch a sports game on television, it is computers that bring us the many different camera angles, instant action replays and tallies of penalties.

Medicine, communication and leisure are just three areas of our lives that have improved because of computers. The advantages they have brought, in my opinion, far outweigh any disadvantages.

Argument Essay

STRUCTURE	Currently, young people in Australia can get their driving licence when they are 17 years of age. There are some very good reasons to raise this minimum age to 19 or even 20. The main reason is that young people are not as mature as older people when driving, and the proof of this is the greater number of young people involved in accidents. However, raising the minimum age will not be enough on its own. There must be better driver education programs for the young, so that when they do get their licences they will be able to drive safely.	**LANGUAGE FEATURES**
Introduction, Which includes: l A lead-in sentence (optional) l A statement of your view on the topic l An 'essay map'		Distance from topic and no emotional language Linking words and phrases
One paragraph per main idea— a topic sentence to show this main idea Development of argument with facts, examples and logical reasoning	Young people do not have the emotional maturity that older drivers generally have. They may be just as good technically. In other words they may be able to drive the car as well as an older person. However, they may not be able to resist peer pressures as well as older people. For example, they might speed or drink-drive to look 'cool' in front of their friends. They are also more likely to take risks that older drivers would not take such not wearing a seat belt or overtaking on a hill. Raising the minimum age would mean that drivers would on the whole be a more sensible and mature group, and there would not be as many accidents.	Occasional use of everyday (colloquial) Words —single inverted commas are used to mark this, e.g. 'cool' Use of pronouns (e.g. 'they') and
At least one paragraph that shows you are aware it is not a black-and-white issue	Every year, approximately 2000 people are killed on Australian roads, and many thousands more are seriously injured. A great number of these people are young adults. In fact, young people aged 15-24 make up 15% of the population but account for 31% of the fatalities (Triggs and Smith, 1996). Although not all these fatalities are drivers, raising the minimum driving age to 19 could reduce these figures.	words such as 'this' and 'these' to link ideas through the text acknowledgement of source
conclusion: l Summarizes essay content l Gives no new information l Restates your view in different words	Changing the driving age would not solve all the problems on our roads. Drivers of all ages cause accidents. I believe that another solution would be to change the laws about driver education programs for all age groups. For example, we could make it compulsory for learners to have a set number of lessons with a registered driving school, instead of learning with friends and relatives. We could also introduce compulsory lessons on the effects of drink-driving and speeding, especially for young people.	Avoidance of 'I" or 'me' in the body, but not always possible in argument essay, e.g. 'I believe' Complete sentences
	Raising the licence age is likely to lower the number of fatalities and injuries involving young people on our roads. Therefore, it should be seriously considered. However, it should not be seen as the whole solution, and should be part of a broader program of change to our driver licensing rules.	

Topic: Do you agree or disagree with the view that the minimum driving age should be raised? (400 words)

Currently, young people in Australia can get their driving licence when they are 17 years of age. There are some very good reasons to raise this minimum age to 19 or even 20. The main reason is that young people are not as mature as older people when driving, and the proof of this is the greater number of young people involved in accidents. However, raising the minimum age will not be enough on its own. There must be better driver education programs for the young, so that when they do get their licences they will be able to drive safely.

Young people do not have the emotional maturity that older drivers generally have. They may be just as good technically. In other words they may be able to drive the car as well as an older person. However, they may not be able to resist peer pressures as well as older people. For example, they might speed or drink-drive to look 'cool' in front of their friends. They are also more likely to take risks that older drivers would not take such not wearing a seat belt or overtaking on a hill. Raising the minimum age would mean that drivers would on the whole be a more sensible and mature group, and there would not be as many accidents.

Every year, approximately 2000 people are killed on Australian roads, and many thousands more are seriously injured. A great number of these people are young adults. In fact, young people aged 15-24 make up 15% of the population but account for 31% of the fatalities (Triggs and Smith, 1996). Although not all these fatalities are drivers, raising the minimum driving age to 19 could reduce these figures.

Changing the driving age would not solve all the problems on our roads. Drivers of all ages cause accidents. I believe that another solution would be to change the laws about driver education programs for all age groups. For example, we could make it compulsory for learners to have a set number of lessons with a registered driving school, instead of learning with friends and relatives. We could also introduce compulsory lessons on the effects of drink-driving and speeding, especially for young people.

Raising the licence age is likely to lower the number of fatalities and injuries involving young people on our roads. Therefore, it should be seriously considered. However, it should not be seen as the whole solution, and should be part of a broader program of change to our driver licensing rules.

Discussion Essay

STRUCTURE Introduction, Which includes: l Lead-in sentence (optional) l Essay question l 'essay map' (no view on question at this stage)	Most people enjoy watching television for information and for entertainment. However, at the same time, they sometimes worry about its influence on their behavior and values. Parents in particular might be concerned about its effect on their children. So, is television a good or bad influence in our lives? Should we consider throwing away our TV sets?	**LANGUAGE FEATURES** The writer keeps a distance from the topic and uses no emotional language Occasional use of questions for dramatic effect
Balanced discussion of issue arguments both for and against — generally one paragraph per argument	There is no doubt that television is an excellent means of education. It allows us to see and learn about people, places and events from all over the world. Nature documentaries are just one example of how TV can do this. Another is news and current affairs programs. People nowadays are far more aware of the politics and cultures of how TV can do this. Another is news and current affairs programs. People nowadays are far more aware of the politics and cultures of distant countries than they were before. This is especially important in countries such as Australia which are so far away from the rest of the world.	Linking words, e.g. 'also', 'however'
Some discussion essays will not be clearly for and against — more a general discussion of ideas	Television is also a great entertainer. With a 'flick of a switch' we can tune into comedies, drama, soap operas, pop music, quiz shows and movies. What's more, this entertainment is almost free. As long as a person has enough to buy or rent a TV set, he or she can enjoy the same entertainment as a multimillionaire.	Non-exist terms
Topic sentences Each paragraph develops one argument with supporting ideas and evidence	Most of the arguments against television are about its ability to influence our behavior. The relationship between violent TV shows influence our behavior, especially for children, is constantly being discussed in the media. Many people claim that TV can directly influence children's behavior, making them violent and aggressive. Others argue that violent behavior in children is more the result of home factors. The evidence is not clear one way or the other, but most parents worry at least a little about the effect of violent TV programs. The recent school violence in the USA has even led President Clinton to call for an end to violence on TV.	Talking about people in general, not individuals, except where it is important to mention an individual, e.g. Clinton Verbs to show what people think and say Complete sentences
	Another argument against television is that it makes very little demand on our brains or bodies. In fact, many people actually use TV to relax and wind down —even to go to sleep by. TV certainly has the potential to stop us doing healthier, more active things with our time. There are even concerns about its effect on conversation and the long-term consequences of this for family communication.	May be reference to 'we' or 'us' to talk in general about 'people' Long nouns
Conclusion: l Summarizes points, gives no new information l Includes a statement of your view on the essay question — for, against or some position in between	Overall, the positive and negative consequences of watching television balance out, and in the end, its effect on our lives comes down to individual use. If we watch TV in moderation, and choose good programs, we can learn from it and get great enjoyment from the entertainment it offers. However, if we let television rule our lives, we may find it does do us harm, both mentally and physically, and then we should think seriously about throwing away our sets.	

Topic: 'We should all throw away our TV sets.' Discuss. (450 words)

Most people enjoy watching television for information and for entertainment. However, at the same time, they sometimes worry about its influence on their behavior and values. Parents in particular might be concerned about its effect on their children. So, is television a good or bad influence in our lives? Should we consider throwing away our TV sets?

There is no doubt that television is an excellent means of education. It allows us to see and learn about people, places and events from all over the world. Nature documentaries are just one example of how TV can do this. Another is news and current affairs programs. People nowadays are far more aware of the politics and cultures of how TV can do this. Another is news and current affairs programs. People nowadays are far more aware of the politics and cultures of distant countries than they were before. This is especially important in countries such as Australia which are so far away from the rest of the world.

Television is also a great entertainer. With a 'flick of a switch' we can tune into comedies, drama, soap operas, pop music, quiz shows and movies. What's more, this entertainment is almost free. As long as a person has enough to buy or rent a TV set, he or she can enjoy the same entertainment as a multimillionaire.

Most of the arguments against television are about its ability to influence our behavior. The relationship between violent TV shows influence our behavior, especially for children, is constantly being discussed in the media. Many people claim that TV can directly influence children's behavior, making them violent and aggressive. Others argue that violent behavior in children is more the result of home factors. The evidence is not clear one way or the other, but most parents worry at least a little about the effect of violent TV programs. The recent school violence in the USA has even led President Clinton to call for an end to violence on TV.

Another argument against television is that it makes very little demand on our brains or bodies. In fact, many people actually use TV to relax and wind down - even to go to sleep by. TV certainly has the potential to stop us doing healthier, more active things with our time. There are even concerns about its effect on conversation and the long-term consequences of this for family communication.

Overall, the positive and negative consequences of watching television balance out, and in the end, its effect on our lives comes down to individual use. If we watch TV in moderation, and choose good programs, we can learn from it and get great enjoyment from the entertainment it offers. However, if we let television rule our lives, we may find it does do us harm, both mentally and physically, and then we should think seriously about throwing away our sets.

Discursive Essay

STRUCTURE		LANGUAGE FEATURES
STRUCTURE Introduction, Which includes: l A lead-in (optional) l Astatement of the issue/topic l An 'essay map'	'In 1900 only one-tenth of the world's population lived in cities. Today, for the first time in history, half the population lives in cities —and in 30 years' time it may rise to as much as three-quarters.' (Rohgers,1998, p.23) Human beings are attracted to the city for many reasons. These include the work opportunities, the entertainment and the services. However, people who live in cities frequently complain about the stress and strain of city life and many talk enviously of life in the country. Clearly there are advantages and disadvantages in both ways of life.	**LANGUAGE FEATURES** Reference to source Distance from topic and no emotional language
Paragraphs organized by the areas being compared or contrasted, e.g. work opportunities	Ever since the Industrial Revolution, people have been coming to cities because of the greater work opportunities. There are more jobs, and a wider variety of jobs, than you are likely to find in country areas, and this is a major attraction of cities especially for young people. Many country towns just cannot keep their youth these days because of the employment situation. However, not everyone who seeks work in the cities finds a job that is satisfying and well-paid. Some people do not find work at all. Unemployment is a problem in the city as well the country, especially if you are young, unskilled and inexperienced.	Formal language, not informal, colloquial language Linking words and phrases to compare and contrast, e.g. 'on the other hand'
Development of paragraphs by comparison and contrast of the two things being examined, i.e. city and country living	There are certainly more entertainment opportunities in the city than in the country. Most urban dwellers have easy access to movies, plays, sports venues, hotels and clubs, whereas country dwellers may have to travel for hours to reach these types of facilities. On the other hand, people in the country have become used to making their own entertainment, and, if they live near a large country town, can probably find as much entertainment as they want.	Word such as 'most', 'may', 'probably' to show awareness that statements may not be true in all cases
Qualifying statements to show it is not a black-and-white issue Topic sentences	There are also more services in the cities. There are many more hospitals, schools, universities and libraries for example. However, nowadays, computer technology is giving country people better access to such services, so the difference between city and country may be decreasing.	Adverbs to show degree of commitment to statement, e.g. 'undoubtedly'
	The lifestyle in the city and country is undoubtedly different. Most city dwellers at some time in their lives get tired of the daily traffic jams, air pollution, and the lack of a community feeling. Many think enviously of the slower pace of the country, the cleaner air, and the greater country to find this. Others know that they would miss the excitement of the city, if they moved away.	Comparative adjectives, e.g. 'cleaner' Complete senteces
Conclusion: l Sums up essay content l Gives no new information l States opinion based on comparison and contrast	In the end a decision to live in the city or country is a matter of personal taste. It will, however, always be a compromise, because neither will ever offer everything a person wants and needs.	

Topic: Is living in the city better than living in the country? Compare and contrast at least three aspects of life to support your view. (450 words)

'In 1900 only one-tenth of the world's population lived in cities. Today, for the first time in history, half the population lives in cities - and in 30 years' time it may rise to as much as three-quarters' (Rohgers,1998, p.23). Human beings are attracted to the city for many reasons. These include the work opportunities, the entertainment and the services. However, people who live in cities frequently complain about the stress and strain of city life and many talk enviously of life in the country. Clearly there are advantages and disadvantages in both ways of life.

Ever since the Industrial Revolution, people have been coming to cities because of the greater work opportunities. There are more jobs, and a wider variety of jobs, than you are likely to find in country areas, and this is a major attraction of cities especially for young people. Many country towns just cannot keep their youth these days because of the employment situation. However, not everyone who seeks work in the cities finds a job that is satisfying and well-paid. Some people do not find work at all. Unemployment is a problem in the city as well the country, especially if you are young, unskilled and inexperienced.

There are certainly more entertainment opportunities in the city than in the country. Most urban dwellers have easy access to movies, plays, sports venues, hotels and clubs, whereas country dwellers may have to travel for hours to reach these types of facilities. On the other hand, people in the country have become used to making their own entertainment, and, if they live near a large country town, can probably find as much entertainment as they want.

There are also more services in the cities. There are many more hospitals, schools, universities and libraries for example. However, nowadays, computer technology is giving country people better access to such services, so the difference between city and country may be decreasing.

The lifestyle in the city and country is undoubtedly different. Most city dwellers at some time in their lives get tired of the daily traffic jams, air pollution, and the lack of a community feeling. Many think enviously of the slower pace of the country, the cleaner air, and the greater country to find this. Others know that they would miss the excitement of the city, if they moved away.

In the end a decision to live in the city or country is a matter of personal taste. It will, however, always be a compromise, because neither will ever offer everything a person wants and needs.

Analytical Essay

STRUCTURE		LANGUAGE FEATURES
Introduction, Which is includes: l A lead-in sentence (optional) l A statement of the issue/topic l An essay map	Worldwide, approximately 10% of all reefs have been degraded beyond recovery, and it is estimated that 20~30% of the world's coral reefs could be destroyed in the next twenty years (International Coral Reef Initiative website). Australian scientists do not want the Great Barrier Reef to be one of these. Unfortunately, however, the coral reefs and other marine life of the Great Barrier Reef are already under serious threat from excess fertilizer and sewage run-off, and from human activity in the area. Two solutions to this major environmental problem are research and education.	Distance from the topic and no emotional language Formal not Informal language Reference to sources
Often a paragraph which defines or describes what or where you are writing about	The Great Barrier Reef is the largest single collection of coral reefs in the world. It is made up of 2000 individual reefs and coral islands, and extends for 2000 kilometers from Papua New Guinea in the north to a point near Gladstone, Queensland, in the south. The reef is vital to the survival of thousands of species of marine life but also to the Queensland and Australian governments because of many tourists who visit it each year.	Pronouns to link ideas through text, e.g. 'this', 'it' Passive voice e.g. 'is made up'
Only information and ideas relevant to essay topic and purpose Organization of ideas by particular l Causes and/or l effects	The reef is rapidly deteriorating due to sewage and fertilizer run-off from the farms on the Queensland coast (mainly sugar-cane farms). The nutrients in the fertilizers and sewage —in particular nitrogen and phosphorus—encourage the growth of algae, which grow rapidly in nutrient-high waters. So, when the waters around the coral reefs become rich in the algae take over and then smoother and kill the coral. The nutrients also stunt the growth of many of the marine animals and plants, and eventually affect the number and diversity of fish, reef-building corals and other sea animals.	Repetition of key words to link ideas in sentences, e.g. 'reef' Adjectives and adverbs to show degree or extent of change, e.g. 'rapidly'
Topic sentences	Another important cause of reef deterioration is tourist activity. Snorkeling, fishing, boating and swimming all contribute to the disturbance of the waters and coral. Fishing, for example, upsets the balance of nature, and boats cause damage with their anchors and their exhaust fumes.	Linking words and phrases, e.g. 'so', 'when'
	One solution to the problem is research. At present tourists are helping to fund research by paying an environmental management charge whenever they enter the marine park (Alcock, 1995, p.27). Another solution is education of tourists and tourism operators, and of farmers. Already this has brought some success. For example, the sugar-cane industry has recently achieved major reduction in its nutrient run-off.	Complete sentences Words to show cause and effect, e.g. 'affect', 'contribute'
Conclusion: l summarizes or refers to essay content l gives no new information l gives a comment of statement of opinion	The Great Barrier Reef is one of the great natural wonders of the world. It is critical to find a solution to the problem of nutrient run-off and human pollution so that the coral reefs and reef marine life are safe for future generations.	

Topic: Choose one environmental problem in Australia. Explain the main causes of the problem and its effects, and outline some solutions. (450 words)

Worldwide, approximately 10% of all reefs have been degraded beyond recovery, and it is estimated that 20~30% of the world's coral reefs could be destroyed in the next twenty years (International Coral Reef Initiative website). Australian scientists do not want the Great Barrier Reef to be one of these. Unfortunately, however, the coral reefs and other marine life of the Great Barrier Reef are already under serious threat from excess fertilizer and sewage run-off, and from human activity in the area. Two solutions to this major environmental problem are research and education.

The Great Barrier Reef is the largest single collection of coral reefs in the world. It is made up of 2000 individual reefs and coral islands, and extends for 2000 kilometers from Papua New Guinea in the north to a point near Gladstone, Queensland, in the south. The reef is vital to the survival of thousands of species of marine life but also to the Queensland and Australian governments because of many tourists who visit it each year.

The reef is rapidly deteriorating due to sewage and fertilizer run-off from the farms on the Queensland coast (mainly sugar-cane farms). The nutrients in the fertilizers and sewage - in particular nitrogen and phosphorus - encourage the growth of algae, which grow rapidly in nutrient-high waters. So, when the waters around the coral reefs become rich in the algae take over and then smoother and kill the coral. The nutrients also stunt the growth of many of the marine animals and plants, and eventually affect the number and diversity of fish, reef-building corals and other sea animals.

Another important cause of reef deterioration is tourist activity. Snorkeling, fishing, boating and swimming all contribute to the disturbance of the waters and coral. Fishing, for example, upsets the balance of nature, and boats cause damage with their anchors and their exhaust fumes.

One solution to the problem is research. At present tourists are helping to fund research by paying an environmental management charge whenever they enter the marine park (Alcock, 1995, p.27). Another solution is education of tourists and tourism operators, and of farmers. Already this has brought some success. For example, the sugar-cane industry has recently achieved major reduction in its nutrient run-off.

The Great Barrier Reef is one of the great natural wonders of the world. It is critical to find a solution to the problem of nutrient run-off and human pollution so that the coral reefs and reef marine life are safe for future generations.

Speech

Topic: Aliens

Aliens

Extraterrestrial beings. Little green men from Mars. Aliens. That's right, ladies and gentlemen. I'm, talking about those unworldly creatures you have all seen in such TV programs as 'Twilight Zone' and 'The X Files', and in such films as E.T. and Close Encounters of the Third Kind.

The big question of course is 'do such creatures exist?' Many would say yes. Many would say no. Those who believe speak of government cover-ups of spaceship landings and conspiracies of silence. The non-believers say that aliens, like magic, monsters and ghosts are only figments of our imagination - pure science fiction.

But I am not here today to prove their existence one way or the other, I want to talk about why we are so fascinated by these creatures - habits we can start to understand the reason for the interest.

Your average alien comes in three types. First, there is the insectoid - a multi-limbed, bug-eyed, praying mantis-like creature. Secondly, there is the reptilian variety, which varies depending on who the director is, but basically it has something of a prehistoric appearance.

But by far the most common is the humanoid alien - a greyish blue or green, short and skinny creature with a huge bulbous head and large eyes. This alien type has no hair, no ears, no nose and only a slit for a mouth. Think Kermit the frog and you have it.

So, what do these guys get up to? Well, here are some of their leisure time pursuits. Firstly - the crop circle. Aliens are said to make these huge circles as they land their spaceships. Are these just young aliens out for a joyride or do these markings have a deeper meaning?

Next, abduction. People are taken or, indeed, beamed up into the spaceship and put through rigorous medical tests and experiments. They are then sent back to Earth to live normal lives and to earn lots of money by selling their stories to newspapers and magazines.

But then we come to the alien invasion. And this is where we Earth people just don't learn. It all starts off with sudden sightings of masses of UFOs looming on the horizon. Do we earthlings prepare for war? No. We all somehow think that the aliens come in peace. But do they ever? No. Again and again, from the H.G. Wells' classic War of the Worlds to blockbusters such as Independence Day, we greet them, show them round and then 'wham bam' - half our population's gone.

But is it perhaps the hope that they come in peace and with interplanetary goodwill that keeps us believing in aliens or, if not believing, at least interested and searching the skies?

Do they exist? Who knows, but I say this. Why not believe in them? Let us prepare for the coming of the aliens, and if they do come, then so be it - we'll be ready. And if they don't, we'll have had a damn good time imagining it all anyway. Thank you.

Matthew Roden

STRUCTURE	**Aliens**	**LANGUAGE FEATURES**
Opening, which quickly catches the audience's attention, and at the same time establishes the topic and purpose of speech	Extraterrestrial beings. Little green men from Mars. Aliens. That's right, ladies and gentlemen. I', talking about those unworldly creatures you have all seen in such TV programs as 'Twilight Zone' and 'The X Files', and in such films as E.T. and Close Encounters of the Third Kind.	Address the audience, e.g. 'ladies and gentlemen', 'class'
	The big question of course is 'do such creatures exist?' Many would say yes. Many would say no. Those who believe speak of government cover-ups of spaceship landings and conspiracies of silence. The non-believers say that aliens, like magic, monsters and ghosts are only figments of our imagination —purc science fiction.	More repetition and restatement of ideas than in writing —to help your listeners follow the ideas
Ideas and information organized as appropriate to purpose of speech	But I am not here today to prove their existence one way or the other, I want to talk about why we are so fascinated by these creatures—habits we can start to understand the reason for the interest.	
Short 'chunks' of information and ideas — divided up in a way which is meaningful to both speaker and listeners	Your average alien comes in three types. First, there is the insectoid—a multi-limbed, bug-eyed, praying mantis-like creature. Secondly, there is the reptilian variety, which varies depending on who the director is, but basically it has something of a prehistoric appearance.	Personal language, e.g. 'I', 'you', 'we', 'us'
Ideas not always fully developed as in an essay	But by far the most common is the humanoid alien —a greyish blue or green, short and skinny creature with a huge bulbous head and large eyes. This alien type has no hair, no ears, no nose and only a slit for a mouth. Think Kermit the frog and you have it.	Often use of humour to keep listeners' attention
	So, what do these guys get up to? Well, here are some of their leisure time pursuits. Firstly —the crop circle. Aliens are said to make these huge circles as they land their spaceships. Are these just young aliens out for a joyride or do these markings have a deeper meaning?	Some colloquial everyday language, e.g. 'guys'
	Next, abduction. People are taken or, indeed, beamed up into the spaceship and put through rigorous medical tests and experiments. They are then sent back to Earth to live normal lives and to earn lots of money by selling their stories to newspapers and magazines.	Use of questions to set up a 'conversation' with listeners
	But then we come to the alien invasion. And this is where we Earth people just don't learn. It all starts off with sudden sightings of masses of UFOs looming on the horizon. Do we earthlings prepare for war? No. We all somehow think that the aliens come in peace. But do they ever? No. Again and again, from the H.G. Wells' classic War of the Worlds to blockbusters such as Independence Day, we greet them, show them round and then 'wham bam'—half our population's gone.	Not always full sentences —phrases and isolated words used for effect
Conclusion, which relates to the content and purpose of the speech, it may include, for example, a question, a recommendation, a warning	But is it perhaps the hope that they come in peace and with interplanetary goodwill that keeps us believing in aliens or, if not believing, at least interested and searching the skies?	
	Do they exist? Who knows, but I say this. Why not believe in them? Let us prepare for the coming of the aliens, and if they do come, then so be it —we'll be ready. And if they don't, we'll have had a damn good time imagining it all anyway. Thank you. **Matthew Roden**	

Research Report

STRUCTURE	Role models for adolescents	LANGUAGE FEATURES
Information organized under section headings	**Aim** The aim of this survey was to discover who were the most influential role models in the lives of a small group of local adolescents. The question was based on a question asked of young people in a much larger nationwide study "The State of Australian Kids' recently conducted by Dangar Research for Kids Helpline.	Formal language Objective not Subjective Language
Headings and formats vary across study areas, but these basic headings are common	**Method** A total of 40 secondary school students between the ages of 15 and 17 were asked the question 'Who is the most influential role model in your life?' All students attended the same school, and there were an equal number of boys and girls in the survey. All subjects were asked the question individually.	focus on facts not opinion although in 'Discussion' a mix of fat and opinion
Each section has a different focus: l Why you did report (aim) l How you did it (method) l What you found out (results) l That you think the results mean (discussion)	**Result** Overall, the most frequent response to the survey question was a parent. Half the subjects said that their mothers or fathers were their role models, with girls slightly more likely to say this than boys. A further eight subjects (four boys and four girls) chose a relative —star— generally a football player. All but one of the five subjects who said this were boys. Three boys chose a singer/musician or an actor. Two girls nominated a teacher, and the remaining two (both girls) each chose a world leader (Nelson Mandela and Martin Luther King).	Passive voice to place emphasis on information not the researcher (you) Few personal pronouns, e.g. 'I' or 'we' Clear, simple language, brief as possible
	Many of those who chose a parent said that they were not always happy with the way their parents disciplined them or restricted their activities, but that most of the time they thought they were 'pretty good' and worth taking notice of in the 'big issues'.	may include some quotes from subjects
results are in order from most important or common to least important or common information organized by paragraphs within sections	**Discussion** The results of the survey are likely to be both encouraging and surprising to parents. Many parents probably believe that they would be the last person their teenagers would nominate as role models, despite secretly hoping that they would. Overall, the responses demonstrate that young people may be more perceptive and discriminating than their parents and teachers believe. They seem able to distinguish between the superficial role models often pushed in their faces by the media (e.g. Hollywood celebrities) and the ones that offer them some serious guidance about life.	Generally pat tense to talk about aim, method and results; present and past tense to discuss results
(longer reports use a numbering system — 2.1, 2.2, 2.3 etc.)	Interestingly, the results quite closely mirrored the findings of the nationwide survey, suggesting that they were not related to the particular location of the school or the backgrounds of the individuals surveyed.	Word such as 'may' and adverbs of likelihood, e.g. 'probably'

Topic: Role models for adolescents

Role models for adolescents

Aim

The aim of this survey was to discover who were the most influential role models in the lives of a small group of local adolescents. The question was based on a question asked of young people in a much larger nationwide study "The State of Australian Kids' recently conducted by Dangar Research for Kids Helpline.

Method

A total of 40 secondary school students between the ages of 15 and 17 were asked the question 'Who is the most influential role model in your life?' All students attended the same school, and there were an equal number of boys and girls in the survey. All subjects were asked the question individually.

Result

Overall, the most frequent response to the survey question was a parent. Half the subjects said that their mothers or fathers were their role models, with girls slightly more likely to say this than boys. A further eight subjects (four boys and four girls) chose a relative - star - generally a football player. All but one of the five subjects who said this were boys. Three boys chose a singer/musician or an actor. Two girls nominated a teacher, and the remaining two (both girls) each chose a world leader (Nelson Mandela and Martin Luther King).

Many of those who chose a parent said that they were not always happy with the way their parents disciplined them or restricted their activities, but that most of the time they thought they were 'pretty good' and worth taking notice of in the 'big issues.'

Discussion

The results of the survey are likely to be both encouraging and surprising to parents. Many parents probably believe that they would be the last person their teenagers would nominate as role models, despite secretly hoping that they would. Overall, the responses demonstrate that young people may be more perceptive and discriminating than their parents and teachers believe. They seem able to distinguish between the superficial role models often pushed in their faces by the media (e.g. Hollywood celebrities) and the ones that offer them some serious guidance about life.

Interestingly, the results quite closely mirrored the findings of the nationwide survey, suggesting that they were not related to the particular location of the school or the backgrounds of the individuals surveyed.

【저자소개】

Hubert H. Pak

Professor
Dept. of English Education
College of Education
Kongju National University
공주대학교 사범대학 영어교육과 교수

****

Boseong Publishing Co.
318-31 Samsung 2-dong, Dong-gu, Daejeon, Korea

First published 2011

ISBN 978-89-6236-065-3 93740

Price ₩15,000